Praise for
*Making the World
Safe for Sorrow*

"*Making the World Safe for Sorrow* is written for all of us who have experienced or are experiencing loss and grief and are questing for wisdom to revitalize our lives. The Reverend Doctor Margaret Izutsu draws upon her lived experience of Japanese cultural practices to make understandable and available for our use a Japanese version of Confucian-tradition rituals that carry the potential to reshape our religious, moral, and aesthetic experiences. Her quest, and the book's achievement, is the result of deep reading into relevant psychological, anthropological, and philosophical literature as well as extensive experience in Japanese culture. Dr. Izutsu provides practical wisdom for the art of living; she illustrates that wisdom with vivid examples from her own experiences and those of parishioners participating in an experimental group. I finished the book and immediately wanted to try the rituals. An appealing and useful way to learn how to transform loss and mourning into cultivation of the self and relationships!"

—ARTHUR KLEINMAN, author, *The Soul of Care*; professor of anthropology, global health, and psychiatry, Harvard University

"An astounding read with loads of resources and suggestions. By sharing insights from the Japanese tradition and inviting the reader to explore learnings from sorrow as well as grieving effectively amid deepening complexities of relationships, this book takes us to depths that bear much fruit. Maggie takes us on her personal journey in ways that invite us to embark on our own and to assist others."

—THE REVEREND DR. MELFORD (BUD) E. HOLLAND, JR., retired from the Presiding Bishop's staff

"*Making the World Safe for Sorrow* is a courageous personal and relational account of the experience of sorrow and the process of grieving. Dr. Izutsu's thesis is that in many Western countries, hyperindividualism prevents people from having a creative, spiritual healing experience of grieving. In effect, without the relational framework that traditional cultural practice—such as Japanese rites for grieving involving public grieving rituals with specified anniversary dates and private meditational ceremonies—an individual cannot fully experience sorrow, mourning, and grief in a constructive, spiritually meaningful way. Dr. Izutsu reviews several psychological, developmental, spiritual, and anthropological sources for her remarkable book. Perusing this book will expand the reader's mind and openness to experiencing a wider range of feelings, including sorrow, and provide a way for sharing these feelings with others—thus grieving in a good way."

—RAY HAWKINS, PhD, ABPP (Clinical Psychology); associate faculty, clinical psychology, Fielding Graduate University; clinical assistant professor, psychology, The University of Texas at Austin

MAKING

THE WORLD SAFE

FOR SORROW

MAKING

THE WORLD SAFE

FOR SORROW

MARGARET W. IZUTSU

GREENLEAF
BOOK GROUP PRESS

This book is intended as a reference volume only. It is sold with the understanding that the publisher and author are not engaged in rendering any professional services. The information given here is designed to help you make informed decisions. If you suspect that you have a problem that might require professional treatment or advice, you should seek competent help.

The names and identifying characteristics of some persons referenced in this book, as well as identifying events and places, have been changed to protect the privacy of the individuals and their families.

Published by Greenleaf Book Group Press
Austin, Texas
www.gbgpress.com

Distributed by Greenleaf Book Group

For ordering information or special discounts for bulk purchases, please contact Greenleaf Book Group at PO Box 91869, Austin, TX 78709, 512.891.6100.

Design and composition by Greenleaf Book Group
Cover design by Greenleaf Book Group and Adrian Morgan

Publisher's Cataloging-in-Publication data is available.

Print ISBN: 979-8-88645-420-8

eBook ISBN: 979-8-88645-421-5

To offset the number of trees consumed in the printing of our books, Greenleaf donates a portion of the proceeds from each printing to the Arbor Day Foundation. Greenleaf Book Group has replaced over 50,000 trees since 2007.

Printed in the United States of America on acid-free paper

26 27 28 29 30 31 32 33   10 9 8 7 6 5 4 3 2 1

First Edition

For my son
May your life be filled with delighting

Contents

"To know something is not as good as loving it, to love something not as good as delighting in it."

—*THE ANALECTS OF CONFUCIUS* 6:20

The Master said: "Put me in the company of any two people at random—they will invariably have something to teach me. I can take their qualities as a model and their defects as a warning."

—*THE ANALECTS OF CONFUCIUS* 7:22

How do we know—with Rilke—
that our part of the meaning of the universe
might not be a rhythm in sorrow?

—*ERNEST BECKER, THE DENIAL OF DEATH*

Note from the Author

For readers unfamiliar with or disaffected by Christian tradition, by the church and/or by "God-talk," in particular, I offer Jewish rabbi and author of *When Bad Things Happen to Good People*, Harold Kushner's very engaging book as a resource: *Who Needs God?* (Summit Books, 2002). One summer, I picked it up at a grocery store and read it on the plane to Japan. Along with the contemporary theologians I cite (such as Walter Wink, Catherine LaCugna, and Richard Rohr) whose revisions of Christian thought have helped me, I'd like to point the reader in the direction of Rabbi Kushner, who proposes that "God" is not a "what"—not a "substance" or a noun—but a "when"—an action, a verb. This fits with my experience of Japan: an emphasis on verbs over nouns, to such an extent that Japanese syntax often omits the subject! It is always inferred, of course—just not as important as the action. Is this evidence of how thoroughly they have embraced getting beyond an ego agenda? I'll let you decide.

Rabbi Kushner cites the spiritual activities that are the basis for that understanding of God: feeding the hungry, clothing the naked, straightening the backs of the oppressed, freeing the captives, and visiting those in prison. Indeed, I am not alone in believing that every generation must work to understand the gospel—or even correct scientific findings and make new imperatives known. The Confucian tradition concurs and has a specific term for this: the rectification of names—calling a spade a spade. What may have passed in an earlier time as one thing can, in a new era, be seen as something else. For instance, I'm thinking of eggs and the warnings about cholesterol back in the day—warnings that likely shortened my father's life—and the revised understanding of how essential eggs are. Primatologist Frans de Waal liberated me from thinking that my mother's parsimoniousness was *my* fault by pointing to the theory in her day of "the over-kissed child," which advised against too much affection, but which came to feel in the next generation as neglect. Adjustments are called for! And such are part of the liberating activities of God, I submit, in which we are co-creators, collaborators, and participants, as well as beneficiaries.

Perhaps this will explain why, in my dedication, for instance, I use the gerund form of the verb ("delighting"), rather than the noun ("delight").

I also want to note that, for Confucian sources, I've used works in translation, as—lamentably—I don't speak Chinese. I hope that, as part of my invitation for further collaboration, if any readers have amendments to my suggestions by virtue of a command of the language and familiarity with primary sources, you'll be sure to let me know!

Finally, please note that Asian names cited are in the traditional Asian order, last names first.

Making the World
Safe for Sorrow

t was in the early 1990s when a tall, slender, elegant, and elderly Episcopalian parishioner planted herself before me as I fumbled with my keys
at the door to my office. It was right after a worship service, and I still
wore my priestly vestments. The woman introduced herself as Ruth and
made a pointed request: "Tell me how to grieve."

I was new at Ruth's church and was serving as a pastoral associate. Some
months before I was hired, Ruth's only son had died in a motorcycle accident at the age of forty, leaving behind his wife and two still-small children.
This was the first time I had spoken to Ruth, but I knew she had probably
heard of the grief support group I'd started at the church. In the group, I
drew on Japanese customs I had come to know during the decade of the
1980s when I'd lived in Japan and married into the culture. During my time
in Japan, I had also worked as an editor, interpreter, teacher, TV "talent,"
and psychotherapist. In the first meeting of the fledgling group, we had
made paper lanterns and floated them on the reflecting pond at the center
of the garden around which the church was built.

Ruth's well-heeled, prim, and proper demeanor suggested to me that the
aesthetics of that exercise would have appealed to her. Having been a cradle

Episcopalian with a father and grandfather who were also priests, I had more than the usual exposure to Episcopalians. And I assumed Ruth was like many. She typified in my mind that unflattering way we Episcopalians often refer to ourselves—God's frozen chosen—so what wouldn't have appealed to her, I imagined, was baring her soul to a group. I understood her request to be for something like a list of "steps" or stages I could just rattle off here in the corridor on the fly and that she could follow without the discomfort of an in-depth conversation, much less that of a group process.

❧

In the decades since Ruth posed that question, she has been, for me, an icon of the lack of knowledge among most Americans about the fundamentals on how to grieve, much less how to grieve effectively. She represented the compounding nature of our tendency to isolate and approach grief as an individual exercise or process. Unfortunately, this tendency to do so without appropriate forms of social support, which are so crucial to the work of grief, can lead to disastrous effects.

In a recent well-researched book on depression and anxiety, *The New York Times* best-selling author Johann Hari uncovered the process toward isolation that Ruth represented. He cited work by Robert D. Putnam, Malkin Research Professor of Public Policy at Harvard University:

> In the ten short years between 1985 and 1994 alone, [Putnam] wrote, "active involvement in community organizations . . . fell by 45 percent." In just a decade—the years of my teens, when I [Johann Hari] was becoming depressed—across the Western world, we stopped banding together at a massive rate and found ourselves shut away in our own homes instead.[1]

Simply stated, "We dropped out of community and turned inward."

Ruth's request seemed to be that I not disturb that "turning inward" inclination. Yet I had become enamored of the deeply social customs surrounding grief that my Japanese in-laws observed and knew how effective they were and could be for Ruth; so I invited her to the group.

After a year of the group meeting weekly, I had an opportunity to go back to study at Harvard Divinity School, where I'd done my master's in divinity. I would focus on a doctoral degree in comparative religion and study more systematically the Japanese rites at the center of my interest and the inspiration for the work I was doing with the group I'd formed. I had started the group with more questions than answers; yet I had a hunch that my fellow Americans might be like me: thrashing about for a vocabulary, syntax, and the stamina to explore the experience of grieving and what it was demanding of us, and what we could learn from it.

Looking back on it now, I was trying to duplicate what I'd been so richly exposed to and nurtured in during my life in Japan: a generous space in which all sorts of thoughts and feelings could be acknowledged without judgment, and a place where we could search for truth and find a way forward based on that. I was lucky to have found congenial friends in Japan who were remarkable at providing this space. When I returned to America, I'd wanted to bring back what I'd learned of these Japanese grieving rites, to supply these practices as something like a seismic souvenir. Or rather, if I can be so bold, as a catalyst to cultural change.

Something went right with that support group I'd formed, despite my ignorance of exactly what I was doing or supposed to do. As I prepared to go back to school, members of the group began to go into the community to act as ambassadors to grieving widows and others who'd experienced a loss—losses that were often so overwhelming that the mourners had become housebound; no doubt this also reflected the American tendency toward isolating. I was delighted, amazed, and encouraged that the members of my group had begun making house calls.

These house calls were definitely countercultural. In the twenty years since Ruth's question, our social connectedness, Johann Hari observed, has plummeted even further. Although an observable trend since the 1930s, Hari wrote that this inclination has "hugely accelerated during my lifetime":

For example, social scientists have been asking a cross-section of US citizens a simple question for years: "How many confidants do you have?" They wanted to know how many people you could turn to in a crisis, or when something really good happens to you. When they started doing the study several decades ago, the average number of close friends an American had was three. By 2004, the most common answer was none.[2]

And recently, Vivek Murthy, who has served several stints as the surgeon general, has declared loneliness a public health crisis: its own epidemic![3] I'd thought the COVID pandemic heightened our awareness of the need for social connection, but it doesn't seem to have changed our habits or mindset or values in any substantial way—not enough, in any case, to stave off the pervasive problem of loneliness to which the surgeon general points. Amid our not knowing how to deal with death and grief, our tendency to isolate seems to create even more suffering.

Did I mention anxiety and depression?[*]

According to Hari, the root cause of anxiety and depression is our isolating tendencies, and the cure is connection. I will argue that what we need goes even deeper than that: We need more than connection, which can remain superficial and futile, or worse. Take the surgeon general's recent warnings about social media, which state that social media is associated with significant mental health harms for adolescents.[4] It's interesting that *the* platform for "connection" clearly has its downside.

Ultimately, due to all our isolating tendencies, modern humans—at least, those of us residing in the United States or perhaps more generally in the West—are alone. And in case you're thinking I'm not giving families their due, Hari notes, "It's not that we turned inward to our families . . .

---

[*] In an interview with Krista Tippett, Andrew Solomon, the well-known author of *The Noonday Demon: An Atlas of Depression*, "traces the onset of his depression from his incapacity to grieve the death of his mother." Krista Tippett, *Einstein's God: Conversations About Science and the Human Spirit* (Penguin, 2010), 228.

we've stopped doing stuff with them, too."[5] And in support of this being "Western world-wide" and not just an American problem, he states, "Virtually all forms of family togetherness . . . became less common over the last quarter of the twentieth century," and there are comparable figures "for Britain and the rest of the Western world."[6]

In a summarizing, pivotal paragraph, Hari states,

> We do things together less than any humans who came before us. Long before the economic crash of 2008, there was a social crash, in which we found ourselves alone and lonely far more of the time. The structures for looking out for each other—from the family to the neighborhood—fell apart. We disbanded our tribes. We embarked on an experiment—to see if humans can live alone.[7]

And this is one of the reasons why Americans struggle with how to appropriately grieve.

As one among myriad examples, my friend Mariah, whose sister died a few years ago, told me over a glass of wine that she was afraid she was not "doing it right," meaning the grieving. Most pointedly, Mariah was afraid the sadness, which she'd learned to manage to a considerable degree, would return with a vengeance. And at that time, she had barely recovered from what she described as "hug rape," which had occurred quite often following the death of her sister. For an extreme introvert like Mariah, being constantly bombarded by well-meaning acquaintances attempting to comfort her with hugs felt like an invasion of her personal space to the *n*th degree, often leaving her panicked and feeling assaulted in her grief-stricken state. A double whammy in her time of mourning.

As many of us now know, there is no one "right" way to grieve; we've heard or read—or unfortunately, experienced—that grief is highly individual and can't be crammed into five stages or even prescribed at all. But that isn't very helpful. Just ask Ruth and Mariah, who were desperately looking for guidance. And the circle expanded: Mariah's cheerful friend, Sunny, approached me for advice about how she could do right by Mariah during the most delicate of grieving phases.

Perhaps you've had your own encounter with this confusion and pain, either as the person directly experiencing a loss or as a friend hoping to offer solace. Which begs the questions: What *are* the experiences you can expect to have in grieving, what support structure is necessary for you to best process grief, and, with any luck, how might you come out the other side stronger and wiser? Perhaps you are someone who's experienced a painful loss, like Mariah or Ruth, whether recently or in the more distant past. If so, I hope you will find in these pages a great deal of relief: a sense of what grief entails—the so-called "work of mourning."

But my equal, if not greater, hope is that all the Sunnys—those looking for ways to be helpful to friends and loved ones adjusting to a loss—also find your own support in this book. My hope is that this book will give you tools to help, not hinder, the grief process. That you'll be better prepared to face your own losses and help others through theirs. That we all grow in our capacity to *be* the social support that grief really relies on but are currently so poorly capable to offer. That we come to understand and supply the contexts most suitable for providing that support. And that we learn to do this well by learning which personal qualities and habits we can cultivate and how to do so.

The Study of Bereavement

In the nearly quarter-century since Ruth's request, lots of work has been done on the subject of bereavement in the United States as we try to figure out just what bereavement *is*, what the tasks are that comprise the "work of mourning," and how best to go about those steps. I will summarize the relevant findings in the next few chapters, but here, I simply want to observe that the situation has not improved much, despite all that work.

When I returned to the divinity school, I was fortunate to be encouraged in my interests in Japanese memorial customs by Dr. Arthur Kleinman, a psychiatrist and medical anthropologist at Harvard, who had a deep concern with the dismal direction that bereavement was headed in the United States. When I first went to see him, he was generous in his willingness to support my application to the doctoral program for the purpose of studying Japanese memorial customs, having done decades of work in China himself.

Dr. Kleinman had also been a member of a prestigious panel of experts led by Marian Osterweis, who'd conducted a groundbreaking study of bereavement in North America in the 1980s.[8] They found that Britain, the United States, and the rest of the Western world are at a loss, stemming from our isolating tendencies and highly individualistic propensities, when it comes to dealing with loss. Their findings included the stunning fact that widows and widowers do worse in the second year after their spouses die than in the first, as measured by a higher morbidity.

Could the Japanese be spared this dismal outcome through the social support they receive due to the pervasive Japanese custom of ritually observing the second anniversary after the death with a gathering of the extended family and close associates—a public social event? This custom is in stark contrast to the common experience of the bereaved in our culture, who find themselves even *more* isolated and *expected* to return to "normal" by the end of the first year, *at the latest*. The Osterweis 1980s study of bereavement in North America had a final recommendation: to conduct cross-cultural, family-based studies of bereavement in non-Western settings involving repeated observations of a cohort over time to discover ways we could do better.[9] And that's exactly what I set out to do.

Under Dr. Kleinman's guidance, I read the medical anthropological material on bereavement across cultures. The result, though, was not especially promising. As I learned more from Dr. Kleinman and groundbreaking anthropological studies from around the globe, my key question crystalized: How do we make the world safe for sorrow? There were dangers to grief—what one major study identified as "the surplus of emotion" and another concerned the "force of emotion."[10] How could we properly channel these forces and excesses to avoid any negative effects? Even if there wasn't *one* "right" way to grieve, I had to hope that surely some ways were better than others.

My experience of the Japanese rites at the center of my research—known as *hōji* (the public, periodic ritual) and *kuyō* (the private, individual ritual, once or twice a day, typically)—is that they do provide both a context *and* structure, the essentials for moving constructively through grief: the *what* there is to be done—starting with a ritual schedule and including various ritual elements, such as prayer, meditation, and contemplation—along with the *how*—with what consciousness or mindset, values, and awareness.

There is a rich body of wisdom literature to guide the participant in cultivating appropriate attitudes as well as behavior, honing one's character as a virtuous person and creating the capacity for being a constructive member of society both in the context of these rituals and beyond. I see now, too, that these resources are about *more* than helping individuals with their grief: They're about creating the kind of culture and society where the surplus and force of emotion are properly channeled and deep communication is possible—one that is ultimately safe for sorrow and makes life worth living. Perhaps it's even more accurate to say that they contribute to making the world safe *from* sorrow.

I realized that the rituals of hōji and kuyō, supported by the culture-wide Japanese habits of humility, responsiveness, and reverence, and robust patterns of interrelatedness, could provide anyone who was grieving the tools, and more specifically the insight, attitudes, and habits to remove the blocks from their own journey through grief and to support others in their grief.

These rites can also help the family and individual rise above a kind of chauvinism that can creep into family affiliations, or even a resurgence of a type of tribal association to move toward an identity with all things:

a profound compassion for and union with all of life. While entomologist E. O. Wilson acknowledges that even humans must belong to a tribe,[11] and Hari writes, "Just like a bee goes haywire if it loses its hive, a human will go haywire if she loses her connection to the group,"[12] our affiliation with life must not stop there. In the words of the Zen abbot who oversaw much of my fieldwork in Japan, the purpose of the ritual, the ideal end or goal, is for the survivors to become "living Buddhas." A living Buddha is able to act from a place of compassion and in union with—not competition with or alienation from—all things. Out of ego *strength* but not with an ego *agenda*. I've included more on striving to become a living Buddha in chapter 4.

The Birth of the Pilot Project

To test the North American adaptability to the Japanese memorial customs I had been so richly exposed to through my Japanese in-laws, I began a pilot project. I have some encouraging initial results from this project that indicate my hope for Americans to embrace better ways to grieve is not entirely unfounded.

In 2009, Jane was in her mid-eighties when she thrust her hand up in response to my canvassing of her congregation for folks who might want to join in an eight-week exploration of bereavement based on the Japanese customs I knew and loved. In the first week of the pilot program, the twelve participants were given some basic instructions about how to create a space for mourning in their home, conduct a simple ritual in that space, and explore ways to approach the ritual—what thoughts, feelings, and actions to consider and cultivate. I asked group members to make notes of questions that arose for them in the context of the ritual.

The plan was to meet every week for seven more weeks—mirroring the first official period of mourning, according to these Japanese customs—to check in with each other and report on our observing the rites. We would discuss how the rites impacted the grief we were experiencing, the difficulties we might be having, whether we'd met our goals or not, or if there were questions the group should consider. I would try to supply answers culled from the body of wisdom literature of the Buddhist, Confucian, and Taoist traditions that undergirded these rites, as well as provide a generous, gracious space for the collective wisdom of the group itself to be expressed. And this, in turn, would help me understand what some basic guidelines might be for Americans wanting to pursue this spiritual discipline or these public rituals on their own.

At our first meeting of her group of six, Jane introduced herself and mentioned a rather fanciful, some might say mystical, experience that had happened six years earlier, when her deceased husband made himself known at a church service some forty days or so after his death. He had been a fireman, and on that day in church, the fire alarm in the chapel began to blare suddenly, unexpectedly, and gratuitously, along with the full array of flashing lights. Jane counted this as a sure sign to her from her husband that he was all right and was now leaving this plane of existence where he'd been hovering since his death.

She referred to that day as the anniversary of his "ascension." Jane may have been prompted to think along these lines following the tradition of the church, as the forty days that had passed since her husband's death aligned with the way the ascension of Jesus is counted from his resurrection and celebrated today in the church calendar. Her experience of her dead husband's presence also aligns positively with the experience of Japanese widows, where eighteen out of twenty of the widows reported the "sense of presence," referred to in bereavement literature as "SOP," of their deceased husbands.[13]

I asked Jane if she'd discussed this episode with her sons. She had three sons from a previous marriage (from which she had also been widowed) and one with her fireman husband. She was taken aback; it had never occurred to her to tell them about it or discuss it with them. Unbeknownst to me at the time, she took this as her homework for the week, and being herself a PhD in education, I was to learn that she took homework assignments seriously! At the next meeting a week later, she reported that she had, in fact, discussed her husband's ascension with all four sons. And to her amazement, the best conversation she had was with her previously unapproachable, fundamentalist-leaning adult child (Jane, herself a stridently progressive, liberal-leaning person).

Others in the pilot project had similar breakthroughs in their realization of personal goals and in getting out of stuck places in their grieving that had plagued them previously. The questions and experiences that emerged from the pilot program, in contrast to Ruth and Mariah's confusion, have come to represent beacons of possibility and promise, hope, renewal, and growth that are facilitated when we attend to our grief appropriately.

To describe the participants' experiences, I begin the first two chapters with a question one participant, Katie, asked: Why do we need these bereavement aids? I then embed others' questions and the way we dealt with them in later chapters. Katie's question has two components: historical and theoretical. In chapter 1, I address the history of memorial rites in the West, beginning with the story of my initial encounter with the Japanese rites I'm inspired by—*my* profound need for them—and their place in an overall ritual schedule that the Japanese follow before describing our loss of ritual resources stemming from the actions of Henry VIII and events in Elizabethan England. In chapter 2, I discuss the psychological theory that has taken up the slack created by the absence of Western ritual and practice, with an eye to the anthropology of grief as well. The psychological and anthropological lines of inquiry are somewhat intertwined and help shed light on where we are and how we got here.

In chapter 3, I describe in more detail the Japanese ritual resources and how they function in Japan, along with their ultimate purpose and method. In chapter 4, I explore the final goal of becoming a living Buddha, and in chapter 5, I explore psychotherapist Mark Epstein's brilliant, original thesis about the origins of Buddhist psychology and philosophy in the historical Buddha's own experience of loss: the death of his mother. Epstein's assertion of an "implicit relational knowing" provides a hopeful and reassuring grounding for our effort to overcome our isolating tendencies.

This sets the stage for me to dive into more of the meat of the matter: the way the pilot participants proceeded, the questions that arose for them, and the answers found in a comingling of wisdom traditions—Confucian, Taoist, Buddhist, and Christian—and out of the depth of the participants' own experiences. In chapter 3, I give you the instructions for performing the same simple rituals as the pilot participants to see what comes up for you (and, for easy reference, I have included them in Appendix A).

For a long time after concluding the pilot project, I delved further into the purpose of the rites and my own understanding of their deeper aims—of the promise these rites hold. I did so by paying close attention to the instruction of my Zen mentor, Head Abbot Fukushima Keido, whose teachings I discuss in chapter 4. Discovering Mark Epstein's work and integrating that with the insights of a few other authors have helped me bridge the cultural gap with Japan and integrate Keido's teachings with the fieldwork I'd done in Japan and the experience of the pilot project participants. I explore this in the rest of the book, starting with chapters 6 and 7.

In chapter 8, I give you concrete suggestions for how to implement all I've outlined in your own life, individually, in a family, and/or in community, whether it's secularly oriented, geographically defined, and/or faith-based. Chapter 9 outlines the work still to be done, the questions still unanswered, and how you might help move us toward a better understanding and mastery of the skill set entailed in grieving.

If you have struggled with what to say to a grieving friend, how to best support them, or agonized over the feelings you yourself have in grief, this book is for you. If you have ever wondered if you're going crazy, or simply wanted to know that you're going to get through it all, this book is for you. And if you wonder what kind of available help there is and how to solicit the help you might need, this book is for you. My hope is that, together, with the simple skills my pilot project participants helped me identify as necessary and in a spirit of collaboration, we can become a culture that creates the space and allows the time necessary for mourning. And for becoming what we truly are and are meant to be.

1

The History of Rites
Gone Awry

first encountered the rituals I am recommending when I was living in Japan.

The year was 1985, and I had just given birth to a large, healthy boy when I fell into a deep postpartum depression. For the first few weeks of his precious new life, I obsessed about giving my son up for adoption, because I felt he deserved so much better than I was equipped to give him. My Japanese in-laws did their best to support my husband and me through that arduous time with our infant son. We sought therapy at a small clinic in Kyoto, my husband's hometown and where I had gone to stay with my in-laws briefly after leaving the hospital with my newborn.

One day in therapy, I burst into tears with the realization of what my maternal grandmother had endured: Her first pregnancy had yielded a stillborn child. My mother was conceived soon after, as a way of forgetting that child.

That child was anything but forgotten, however. My grandfather, who was ninety-five and living in Columbus, Ohio; my mother, living in metropolitan

Detroit; and I, on the other side of the world, were all thinking about that child on the occasion of the birth of my own, so many decades later.

When my son was eight months old, I took him with me on a visit to my parents back in the States. My grandfather was visiting at the same time, which was perfect, as I wanted to know more about his experience with his first child. I took my grandfather out to lunch to see what I could learn.

I chose a fancy restaurant. We sat down at a table draped in white linen and placed our orders. After the salads arrived, I asked my grandfather to tell me what he could remember about the birth of his first child.

He shoved his plate away. "Terrible salad," he declared. I suppose he reached for his Bloody Mary. I was so stunned that I didn't notice. What I did see was that his grief was as raw as those lettuce leaves. And that that was the end of the conversation.

I suppose my grandfather's enraged silence on the subject of his dead child is one of the reasons that I have been dedicated to developing a vocabulary and syntax for talking about grief. But I've also understood that we need stamina—emotional strength—as well. Maybe my grandfather had a vocabulary and syntax but lacked stamina. Or perhaps he had stamina but lacked the words. We will never know. Three years later, he went to his grave with whatever feelings and thoughts he'd ever had about his first child, as far as I know, unuttered and forever so.

What I do know is that often the two—stamina for and a vocabulary about experience—grow hand in hand. The attempt to put feelings, thoughts, and experiences into words creates stamina, and the opposite is also true: The development of stamina leads to further articulation—the ability to "name it and tame it."

Perhaps, then, most of all, we need a context: the time and space for developing both the stamina and the vocabulary and syntax to talk about grief. Francis Weller, psychotherapist and author of *The Wild Edge of Sorrow: Rituals of Renewal and the Sacred Work of Grief*, identifies that our need is to apprentice ourselves in grief.[1]

This is where Japanese ritual life comes in.

My own stamina in the face of the mildly violent reaction of my dear granddaddy was, I suspect, the result of my having already conducted the rites for the child I had hoped to learn more about. That came about in an indirect way. Or perhaps the more appropriate way to describe it is as a kind of "all roads leading to Rome" convergence of experience, pressure points, and paths.

Let me go back to the situation of my dawning awareness of what my grandmother had been through and the way my therapy proceeded. I still remember having been flooded with empathy for what it must have been like, in my crude characterization of my grandmother's experience to have given birth to death instead of life. *How devastating and how terrifying*, I thought, with visceral sympathy. But I knew I could only begin to imagine what she had felt and thought.

I was plagued by a kind of survivor guilt, a gut-wrenching remorse for having what she had been so cruelly deprived of herself—a baby that was born alive and well. Most of all, I realized I saw my grandmother as a woman in her own right for the first time. And it made sense of a dream I'd had in my first round of therapy, years before I got pregnant with our son, when I had struggled mightily with clinical depression. In the dream, my husband was teaching me the lyrics to the Barbra Streisand song "Evergreen" from *A Star Is Born* before I was to go out on stage to perform it. On my way to the stage, I had to walk past a chain-link fence that enclosed a barren playground with a casket in the middle of it, around and around and around which a petite elderly woman paced with her head bent down, her whole body hunched over. The casket was open and facing away from view but exuded a bright, effulgent light, which the elderly woman seemed not to notice for all her focus on the dirt ground and her obsessive rounds around it. I never made it onto the stage; I was immobilized and transfixed at and by this barren site.

When I was growing up, my mother was nervous about "dwelling" on things, and I confess, it bugged me. It felt as if she were avoiding something—something very important that would be helpful to talk about. Her own mother's obsession with the death of her first child likely deprived my mother of a certain degree of maternal preoccupation that *she* was due when she came into the world. I do know that my mother was treated with kid gloves, I suppose for fear of losing *her*—in whom so much was now invested: both her own worth and her role as a substitute for the child who never lived.

Still, there must be a middle ground, I thought, *between obsessively feeling nothing but grief and its complete opposite, refusing to even dare consider one's grief for fear of inappropriately "dwelling" on it.* There must be a way through this impasse, to attend to the feelings and the tasks of mourning that would eventually allow one to perceive the light, that bright, effulgent beam of it. To get on with life, to get to the stage where one "performs," where one has a chance to shine. To become one with that bright, effulgent light.

I pondered this back at our tiny home in Japan, sitting with my new baby after a brief stint staying with my in-laws. I was deeply depressed, and while in my own obsessive loop, I happened upon a TV segment of an afternoon talk/variety show that featured a discussion of Japanese memorial rites. The hosts of the *Wide-Show* touted the rites for mourning those people who had died but had not yet been properly mourned. I vaguely recall that they ascribed to the souls of the unmourned dead some disturbing traits, like their need to be grieved and their resulting aggressive, but often misunderstood, efforts to get our attention "from the other side," as it were, by causing us misfortunes and the like . . . or maybe I picked that up somewhere else along the line, for it surely is a common belief in Japan.

In any event, during my next walk with our family dog along a gorgeous mountain ravine, I began my own rumination on all of this, imitating what I had been contemplating. We passed by a neighbor who happened to be outside tending her garden, and I mentioned my interest in these rites and the reason for it.

My neighbor looked uncannily like both my actual grandmother and the elderly woman in my dream: petite, wrinkled, with a small face, although my neighbor wasn't hunched over. It would've been impossible for me to imagine then that the bright spirit I spoke to on that day would be buried alive ten years later when the mountain behind her house collapsed on her during the Kobe earthquake. But on the day of my walk, she kindly invited me inside her house. After hearing my story, she agreed that I should burn an offering for the peaceful repose of the agitated spirit of my stillborn aunt. She fetched a small container of ash from her hibachi in an inner room, which would hold the sticks of incense, and told me how to go about it.

I remember that first offering so well. I commandeered a small dining room window that had been glassed in after the removal of an air-conditioning unit. This put my little makeshift altar at eye level, helpfully out of range of either the jumping dog or crawling infant. Before now, prayer had always seemed to be a matter between God and me—a personal piety in a strictly vertical dimension or line. This strikes me as odd when I think of it now, because we in the Episcopal Church *always* prayed for others. Some of my own ancestors (including my father) had been deeply involved in the so-called "social gospel" movement in the '60s and '70s—working for open housing, championing civil rights, and even starting the abolitionist movement, which was credited to a great-uncle several generations ago.

But there, experiencing that little private ritual, the barren area all around me, made so by a too stringently privatized religion emphasizing my connection with God and my conscience—an almost exclusively vertical dimension—was suddenly filled in on the horizontal plane. I didn't understand it at the time, but I suppose we could say that the world of souls and my relationship with them that had so long been forgotten or sidelined, minimized, dismissed, or repressed, had gained access to the living again, at last. In other words, the horizontal plane of relationships with the dead—deeply diminished by our casual, nonexistent, off-handed, or abstracted memorializing of them—was now full again. I remember feeling something I'd never felt in prayer before: satisfaction. I can honestly say I didn't even know that such a feeling existed in relation to prayer.

Previously, I hadn't known that satisfaction resulting from prayer was even a remote possibility.

The rite itself was simple: lighting a candle from which, in turn, I lit a stick of incense; I may have made little offerings of rice and water, too. I put my hands together, clapped twice, and bowed in prayer, mumbling a petitionary phrase for the peaceful repose of my aunt. I then raised my head, clapped twice again, blew out the candle, and left the incense to slowly spend itself in a rising tendril of aromatic smoke.

This basic, common ritual that made such an impact on me is known as kuyō and is observed in most homes in Japan. It may be performed once or twice a day. And kuyō was at the core of the initial instructions I gave my pilot project participants as we set out to explore together their ability to grieve and their mourning process. My fundamental question was: How did their experience of these Japanese rites affect their grieving?

I began with the basic framework of the ritual as I've described my experience of it to you here: The participants had enough to work from, but I didn't give them *too* much or make suggestions in any coercive fashion so that they would feel oppressed by it or hampered in their creative adaptation of it. (See Appendix A for the basics of what I told them.) They were free to do as much or as little as they wanted; it was their reasoning for what they did or did not do that was of paramount interest to me.

The two principles I followed are core to the Anglican tradition: In worship (or "liturgy," the "work of the people"), there is to be no coercion, *ever*; and *lex orendi, lex credendi*: What we believe arises out of and becomes codified from how we find ourselves naturally falling into praying. Our creeds—or various doctrines and dogmas—are simply how we make sense of our experiences, which, ideally, are spontaneous, "Spirit-filled," and holy, not domineering, violent, competitive, or imposing. To the extent that the church has participated in these latter aggressive qualities, embraced them, or exhibited them, it has lost its way. I hoped that my work with this group might offer a modest bit of a corrective to all of that.

I also hoped that the design of this experiment and experience would enable me to learn which aspects of the Japanese tradition would be comfortable, comforting; which might need explanation to become an attractive option, and what explanations I could give that would be useful in overcoming cultural barriers or personal prejudices, so that these resources were accessible, at least, and effective, at best.

This is how I explained the purpose of the pilot project when I first met with the pilot project participants. At the outset of our eight-week series of meetings, my twelve pilot project participants, unequally divided into three separate groups, were middle- and upper-class White folks who were mourning a variety of losses or seeking a new spiritual practice. They had all the telltale signs of the death-denial of our culture and the toll it takes: They looked anxious, skeptical, weary. Behaviorally, in addition to being basically friendly, open, and seeking, they could be diffident, defensive, and mildly aggressive. But over the course of our work together, modeled on the Japanese memorial customs I'd learned to love, both hōji (the public ritual for extended family) and kuyō (a private, often personal ritual conducted in the home, either by one or only a few more immediate family members), the group not only began to relax into the work but delighted in learning from each other, and I from them.

As the pilot project participants settled into our weekly routine of reporting on our experiments with the rituals and how these resources were affecting their experience of their grief, Katie spoke up. Katie was a recently remarried, middle-aged professional woman who was mourning the very public and tragic death of her brother. She asked why we were even doing all this, answering my own question of what Americans wanted or even *needed* to know about these rites. Katie's query was a rather stark one, much like Ruth's pointed request to be told how to grieve.

Though Katie said there was no doubt in her mind that she needed our group and wanted to be there, she still wondered what had led to our collective need to band together like this, trying on another culture's means of facilitating grief. She asked how we came to be without bereavement aids.

I understood this as a historical query, and so I gave the participants some historical context.

Purgatory, Priestly Corruption, and Kingly Sovereignty

At Katie's question, my mind went immediately to the words of noted Shakespearean scholar Stephen Greenblatt. He'd been presenting a paper that would be the basis for his future book, *Hamlet in Purgatory*.[2] Making no bones about the arduousness of the historical research, Greenblatt described in some detail how he'd uncovered the contentious debate that raged in Tudor England over the Roman Catholic Church's practice involving indulgences or suffrages.

The controversy over indulgences was essentially about the practice of mourners paying priests to say masses for the dead with an eye to shortening the time that the deceased would spend in purgatory, heaven's antechamber. This custom was prevalent during the rule of King Henry VIII and added money and memorial customs to the combustible mix of Henry's misgivings about Rome's influence in his domain. I love telling the story of Henry VIII's involvement in all this. Poor Henry. He is so vastly misunderstood. The business about wanting to divorce his wife leading to a schism with the church: That's true, on the face of it. But the greater issue for Henry, as I understand it, was his sovereignty. No one, especially the pope, was going to tell him what to do in his own country.

Greenblatt had uncovered Simon Fish's anonymous tract addressed to Henry entitled *A Supplication for the Beggars*, a vehement plea concerning the increasing impoverishment of the general populace due to the church's massive sales of indulgences. Fish was also concerned about priestly peddled superstition regarding the afterlife that had paralyzed the public's imaginations in paroxysms of fear. Fish passionately petitioned Henry on behalf of the poor and of England. In the end, Henry VIII banned all mention of the concept of purgatory.

Greenblatt's point in recounting this whole history is to show us that Shakespeare was even *more* of a genius than we'd previously thought. Greenblatt revels in Shakespeare's ability to structure an intricate play— *Hamlet*—around this now troublesome notion, purgatory. Shakespeare escapes the king's censors by never actually uttering the word "purgatory" in the script, instead embedding purgatory's schema in the very fabric of the performance so that theatergoers could have one last cathartic experience of the consolations of this elaborate system.

My favorite example is the scene in the king's chambers where Hamlet has an opportunity to take revenge for his father's murder. Hiding behind the drapes in the king's bedroom, sword in hand, he sees Richard—his usurping uncle—as he kneels in prayer at his bedside. But Hamlet is thwarted by his realization that if he kills Richard while he's at prayer, the usurper king will go straight to heaven—which is far from what Hamlet intends! The implication being, of course, and as the audience will surely know, that Hamlet's hope is to prolong Richard's sojourn in purgatory, if not send him straight to hell.

This was as much as I knew at the time of the pilot project. And it was enough to satisfy Katie—and probably almost anyone else in the Episcopal Church, as we're part of the Anglican tradition, created by Henry VIII himself when he split with Rome. As Episcopalians, we are very conscious of our origins with Henry VIII, and within the Anglican tradition itself, there is a so-called self-appointed "low church" faction (with emphasis on simplicity of ritual), its chief characteristic being an explicit disdain for "Romish" customs like incense and other elements of ritual practice (ruefully referred to as "smells and bells"). I was raised in that tradition of simplicity, which nonetheless retained an appreciation for elegant ritual, along with the historical disdain for Romish customs. But it had never occurred to me that a whole *set* of rituals was done away with as a result. The focus of much of low-church Anglican revulsion toward Roman customs has always been on the corruption of the Roman Church, the exploitation of the poor beleaguered believers through fearmongering. Yet this Anglican branch completely failed to see, much less provide an alternative to, what we *deprived ourselves of* as a result of the split with Rome.

In the context of understanding the historical origins of our *need* for help with our mourning—which we now understand is an ongoing, long-term process—our loss of the imaginary construct of purgatory comes into sharp focus and highlights the void its loss created.

Both Greenblatt's book and that of historian Richard Fenn argue that, despite Henry VIII's fervent intention to rid his land of the Romish notion, Anglo-American culture at large is still heavily influenced by the doctrine and practice of purgatory—even if not consciously. While Greenblatt mostly laments what's gone missing, Fenn is focused on what took shape as a result. According to Fenn, the ban on purgatory didn't eradicate the notion altogether, but rather caused it to go underground from whence it has had a pervasive, pernicious, and enduring effect on American culture—even to the extent of helping to form the American character. Greenblatt's and Fenn's work help explain why I felt that private moment of satisfaction at my little Japanese altar and with it a sense of retrieving something that had gone missing.[3]

Several things these historians notice help us understand what took up the slack—however imperfectly—for the purgatorial rituals no longer available and the mandate for looking into other sources of help for our grieving.

A closer reading of Greenblatt's book moved me, particularly the author's revelation that his own father left money for kaddish to be said for him, apparently not trusting his own sons to perform that Jewish duty. *Kaddish*, for readers unfamiliar with the term, refers to the "Mourner's Kaddish"—a ritual prayer said only in a minyan, or a group of ten adults, praising God as an act of ultimate faithfulness despite the pain of loss. A far superior assertion of one's faithfulness, I believe, than the Protestant admonition to cheerfulness, which carries a strong potential for suppressing, or even complete dissociation from, sadness and sorrow and their appropriate expression. The Mourner's Kaddish is recited over a duration of time, depending on the relationship, far longer than the funeral provisions of mainline Protestant denominations, but still falling far short of the unending schedule of memorial customs followed by the Japanese.

Greenblatt uncovered documents that suggest Shakespeare's *own* father made arrangements for masses to be said upon *his* demise and surmises that Shakespeare's father was Catholic in Protestant England, with all its own attendant deprivations and oppressions. Greenblatt's noting of the senior Shakespeare's distrust of his sons indicates, perhaps, that the dissolution of familial ties that Hari documented, which I discussed in the introduction, began even before we realized and affected even more than we knew.

Greenblatt also noticed that Shakespeare's own *son*—Hamnet—had died five or six years before *Hamlet* was penned, lending a personal ache and longing to the exploration Shakespeare makes of the purgatorial landscape embedded in the play. All of this suggests that we have felt—and regretted—the lack of adequate means for mediating our mourning—and have roughly compensated for that deficit—for a *very* long time.

Perhaps it is this history that Thomas Lynch, an Irish undertaker turned writer, poet, and star of the powerful PBS documentary *The Undertaking*, had in mind when he described our current situation with respect to bereavement in a review for *The New York Times* Book Review in 2006. Now living and working in Michigan, Lynch describes Americans as: "ritually adrift, metaphorically impoverished and existentially vexed."[4] He attributes this to our having severed "communal, ethnic and religious ties" and to our confusion over "the changing mythologies of extinction," or views on death. For now, let me address the problem of poetics—the metaphorical impoverishment that Lynch notices—with Greenblatt's help.

But first, let me observe one last thing I appreciate about *Hamlet in Purgatory*, and that is Greenblatt's refusal to demonize the Roman Catholic Church. To be sure, things got out of hand. And his discussion of the lousy theology that allowed that to happen is informative. I had thought the purgatorial schema had placed a mistaken emphasis on "works": the ability to "earn" our salvation. Christian theology has long eschewed this wrong-headedness, seeing salvation as a matter of *grace*—nothing that I or anyone else can do to bring about or will ever "merit," and that includes being able to pay for it. But Greenblatt points out that the discussion in Henry's day centered more on the gracelessness of the church! Indeed, as a matter of grace, how does the church justify charging exorbitantly for it?

The Poetry—Not Place—of Purgatory

But even prior to that discussion, Greenblatt extolled the "poetry of purgatory," asserting the original intent of the purgatorial schema was *not* to extort or exploit, much less name an actual "physical" place: It was simply an imaginative attempt to manage the terror common to us all. The fear, if not of dying, at least of the dead.

Purgatory was not initially a *place* at all, much less a place one went to after death. It was a poetic prop for preparing for one's *own* death and mourning the loss of those we love. What we lost through Henry's ban on purgatory—or, perhaps, what was lost even *prior to* Henry's ban—was a mooring in poetic sensibilities—an ability to work—or play—with images and metaphors, to be free to see oneself in a variety of ways without undue fear imposed from the outside, an institution taking advantage of one's inherent terror. Displacing the earlier notion of purgatory as a metaphor, an imaginative construct understood as simply that—a function of the imagination—it became a literal place. This literalism opened the way to rigidity, abuse, oppression, and exploitation, which were bound to show up somewhere, somehow. And the impoverishment of the English people was thereby not only financial or monetary, but, more devastatingly, emotional, psychological, spiritual, relational, and communal.

Strengthening Greenblatt's contentions is a contemporary cross-cultural study of grief, which found three things to be universal: fear of the corpse, anger, and crying or keening.[5] Yet Philippe Ariès, in his magisterial tome *The Hour of Our Death*, likes to think that death, in fact, was not always feared. In a perhaps romantic gloss on what he terms "ancient death"—the way death was once anticipated, prepared for in company with family, and welcomed—he creates the foil for the rest of his exploration of how death has been approached since roughly 1000 AD.[6]

Written in 1981, *The Hour of Our Death* deeply laments our shunting death off to the medical profession. Philippe Ariès noted that our inability to talk about death resulted in the return of the macabre—which had been ubiquitous in the Middle Ages and showed up again in early modern times in the form of memento mori (the custom of photographing dead children, for instance, as a memorial practice) but had gradually disappeared. Ariès sees the macabre creeping back into our lives in the form of tubes and medical technology and getting in the way of our human companionship in the last hours we spend on earth.

When Ariès discusses purgatory, he notes the preference that began in the fourteenth century for burial not in collective cemeteries, but rather in well-traversed locations, with inscriptions begging the passerby to pray for him. He sees this as a result of the emphasis on soliciting prayers from the living after death and views it as a historical precedent toward our individualistic tendencies and our grasping at straws for fame, rather than finding comfort through immersion in a network of ongoing relationships.[7]

Of course, there is no mention of purgatory in the Bible, and even though early Christian theologians—Origen in the third century, Gregory the Great in the sixth—made passing comments that bear the mark of the future imaginative construct, it did not take hold until the twelfth century, with its heyday coming in the sixteenth and seventeenth centuries during the Counter-Reformation.

And though Greenblatt acknowledges that we must address the abuses to which purgatory succumbed, he laments what was lost with the ban on purgatory:

> Purgatory enabled the church to make sense of . . . reports [of hauntings], to harness the weird and potentially disruptive

psychic energy to its liturgical system, and to distinguish carefully between those experiences that could be absorbed into the
moral order (encounters with "good" ghosts) and those that had
to be consigned to the sphere of the demonic. The notion of suffrages—masses, almsgiving, fasts, and prayers—gave mourners
something constructive to do with their feelings of grief and
confirmed those feelings of reciprocity that survived, at least for
a limited time, the shock of death. Moreover, the church could
find in Purgatory a way to enable mourners to work through,
with less psychological distress than they otherwise might experience, their feelings of abandonment and anger at the dead. To
imagine the dead in great pain no doubt caused alarm, fear, and
pity, but it also served other, murkier needs, needs that could
be resolved in organized acts of mercy or even in the delay or
withholding of organized acts of mercy.[8]

Greenblatt also emphasizes that it is not simply the loss of purgatory
and its associated rituals that is at stake—the loss of which we still suffer
from deeply, as evident in Ruth, Mariah, and Sunny's requests, along with
the pilot project participants—for guidance in grieving. He writes, "Th[e]
dispute over Ophelia's funeral ceremony is an instance of an overarching
phenomenon in *Hamlet*: the disruption or poisoning of virtually *all* rituals
for managing grief, allaying personal and collective anxiety, and restoring
order" (emphasis added).[9]

It was not just the rituals that got deleted. Along with the disappearance
of rituals went the idea of and the support for the time it takes to grieve and
also to prepare for one's own death, the structure and guiding ideals for
cultivating one's character more generally, and a social setting or support
for it all.

For Katie, the absence of a fixed schedule for ongoing grief opened
her to criticism from people closest to her for "still" mourning the loss
of her brother a year later. In the Roman tradition, beyond the purgatorial

schema, she would have had access to the "Month's Mind"—rituals for marking the first month after the death—and an annual mass to be said for the dead. Instead, as an Episcopalian, she has been left, as undertaker Thomas Lynch observed, "ritually adrift, metaphorically impoverished and existentially vexed."[10]

Greenblatt also does a remarkable job of showing us the flotsam and jetsam that resulted from the shipwrecked notion of purgatory: the difficulty of disentangling the charitable institutions from the church. This necessitated finding other sources of financial support for the beneficiaries of indulgences, such as schools, hospitals, and orphanages, which had been built as a means of releasing one's loved one from purgatory by underwriting good works.

Without the notion of purgatory, and as I alluded to earlier, Protestant preachers admonished mourners to "be cheerful." After all, their loved ones had gone on to heaven, so there was really nothing to mourn. To be sad was seen as a sign of a lack of faith. As a result, sorrow was crowded out along with the idea of purgatory and buried with the dead in a rush to the resurrection that had no patience with grief. This left only an empty, aching stoicism within—and among—mourners.

The loss of purgatory and its accompanying rituals not only destabilized society and the institutions it underwrote, but, without any established means for channeling the "surplus" and "force" of emotion that had been available through the purgatorial rituals, we're not at all sure how to go about grieving. Shakespeare shows this clearly as we witness Hamlet's enormously difficult transition from "revenge" as a regression to the most ancient means of mourning to "remembrance" as the new mandate. Without the structure and tasks entailed in purgatory, all the surplus and force of emotion arising in bereavement had to go *somewhere*, and a regression to a vengeance mindset seemed natural and unavoidable.

Hamlet oscillates between the tried-and-true, impulsive vengeance mourning and this new form of remembrance mourning. The play registers concern over Hamlet's inability to act—to take revenge—but also, I suspect, recognizing the difficulty of remembering without adequate forms of support and guidance for this type of mourning—how to do it wisely, not obsessively like my granny, as depicted in my dream, going round and round a casket without end. Or clumsily, like Mariah's friends who, in her view, committed "hug rape." Not to mention, Hamlet is all alone and going against the tide. His insanity is feigned, but not Ophelia's, and many a person newly bereaved wonders if they might be going crazy. And this state of mind is certainly not encouraging for a full remembrance and a fair rendering of those we are grieving. And is remembering even enough, especially when viewed against the relinquished relishes of revenge?

Like Hamlet, all of us, having lost the supportive rituals of purgatory, are in a transitional state—caught between revenge and remembrance as the proper tasks in mourning. We are all a little bit lost. And the regressive urge for revenge is all around us. No wonder Ruth was looking for guidance, Mariah was afraid she wasn't doing it "right," and Katie was unclear about why—historically speaking, but perhaps echoing an even deeper concern, perhaps that existential vexation that Lynch notices—we needed to seek new resources for grieving in the first place.

Our Relationship with Time

I want to turn to Richard Fenn's provocative essay *The Persistence of Purgatory* for his reflections on remembering. He observed more generally that "the act of remembering . . . is a way of reconstituting the self; old love returns, and in its warmth the soul's own self-feeling is rekindled."[11]

I find this type of remembering quite prominent in the performance of the Japanese rituals of hōji and kuyō. I've experienced this rekindling of love of the deceased many times, which then contributes to a good feeling about oneself. In addition, simply having something to *do*, in our proactive culture, might help mitigate the pervasive sense of helplessness and powerlessness that often accompanies the experience of loss; Greenblatt points out that the ban on purgatory and its rituals deprives us of having something constructive to do even with "the murkier" feelings, perhaps guilt, or the kind of ambivalence Freud was deeply aware of and concerned about, as I discuss in the next chapter. Ultimately, I feel that the rituals' power for stirring up feelings of love and care—an actual *experience* of those emotions—is much more efficacious than platitudes of how the deceased go on "living in our memories" or "our hearts."

Even when a person's relationship with the deceased is ambivalent, complicated, and difficult, the rituals provide a structure for that relationship to evolve—for feelings to shift or mellow, for insight to arise, for a change to occur. My dissertation research subject—a close friend of mine who'd had a deeply strained relationship with her now deceased mother-in-law—began the rituals with her mother-in-law's photo *not* in the altar facing her, as would be the custom, but *behind* my friend, way above the door! Yet gradually, as life with her surviving father-in-law showed her that *he* was the true source of much of her distress, my friend developed a new empathy for her mother-in-law. And day by day, my friend moved the photo closer to and finally resting on the altar, where it normally would be. This potential for a change in perspective, for recovering lost insights or feelings, offers yet another reason to institute a practice that embraces these rituals. This change in mindset might even help diminish the depression and anxiety that are so pervasive in today's society.

Performing rituals can be a double-edged sword, to be sure. Sometimes, enlisting the help of others in the public ritual of hōji is needed to offset the one-sidedness of the personal practice of kuyō. And vice versa: a nurse at the hospice where I did fieldwork in Japan told me she needed her personal practice of kuyō to recover her agency when her relatives chided her for being unmarried at the public hōji for her parents.

One family I worked with suffered a kind of intergenerational trauma when the mother—a replacement child, a phenomenon I've identified in relation to my own mother—attempted unilaterally, with no family discussion, to "honor" her dead father's memory and last wish by destroying an agreement that she had insisted her three children enter into decades before related to the disposition of his property upon his death. This distorted loy-alty to the dead damaged the children's ability to trust her and each other, hurt them badly, and, not to mention, perpetrated dysfunction that had begun generations earlier. It would appear her own mother paid insufficient attention to her needs—those of the living—out of too much attention (but not of a helpful kind) to the dead—much like my granny, obsessed with the death of her stillborn child. Readers familiar with generational trauma may recognize this as a species of that intergenerational distress.*

Yet Richard Fenn's central concern is not with our enthrallment to the dead through a thoughtless obedience to their wishes, but rather with our relationship to time. Fenn observes that along with purgatory, and partly because of it, time acquired a new significance from the eleventh century onward. Our concern with time was molded by the need, according to the doctrine of purgatory, to make the most of our time on earth so as to limit the time spent after death in purgatory. But our relationship with time was also affected by the invention of clocks and watches and organizations, starting with the church, but extending to guilds and industry of all kinds, which began to exert a claim on the way individuals spent time. "The more one's activities are governed by an organization," Fenn writes,

> the less they are governed by one's needs or moods, by the times
> suitable for personal relationships with others, by the natural
> seasons, by anniversaries of public and private events, and by
> aspirations for a future that could ennoble the present and trans-
> form one's existence.[12]

---

* The mother of my example having been a so-called "replacement child" was a kind of hom-age to the dead at the expense of the living—a recognized phenomenon in the bereavement literature. Her wings were literally as well as figuratively clipped out of fear of losing her too: Her parents indulged her longing to learn how to fly, only to the extent of sending her to ground school, provided she never took off! In the case of her own children, this mother's honoring the wishes of her dead father replicated a kind of "clipped wings" phe-nomenon, as the relationships between them were blighted by distrust engendered in the process of fulfilling the wishes of her deceased father. And wreaked havoc in what other-wise might have been long-established good-faith relationships among the living.

These historical factors helped explain not only where we are with our grieving and what has brought us here, but also something about Katie's specific experience. Katie was acutely attuned to what psychologists call "the anniversary phenomenon." On the first-year anniversary of her brother's death, Katie felt inclined to do something to commemorate it. As I mentioned before, she was met with stiff opposition from people closest to her. Her isolation and pain were only intensified by the fact that sibling loss is already a routinely disenfranchised grief. Katie found great solace and validation in the fact that the Japanese rituals provided for a public memorial event on the first and second anniversaries, along with a sporadic host of others.

Without this structure and social support for grieving, however—lost in the West through rituals abolished when purgatory was banned and additionally burdened by new, secular pressures on time—Fenn observed that this has bled over into all areas of life and that people will seek "shamans and priests" to tell them what to do and when. And *this* explained why some of my closest friends have sought mediums in the process of their bereavements, and why Mariah and her friend Sunny sought me.

Fenn was deeply disturbed by the effect that a new relationship with time had on individuals. Such external demands, he says, ultimately result in people in the West having lost a sense of their own being. He dubs this "soul-loss." In place of a soul, the modern "self" emerged. He notes that contemporary philosopher Charles Taylor observed that "reflexivity"—the ability to think about oneself—developed initially in conversation between the living and the dead, and that "the modern self emerged as Westerners began to lose their sense of being in spiritual conversation with unseen spirits and with departed souls."[13] Without this mooring, individuals began to feel increasingly responsible for their own souls, while this actually created detachment for people from their immediate experience.

We saw this detachment from the spirits and how it affects immediate experience in one pilot program member's weekly check-ins with the group. Jenni was mourning the death of her father, a scientist like herself, so she set up an altar where she made offerings and attempted to engage her father. Yet Jenni reported quite dismissively to the group that she'd "just" (as in "merely") had a conversation with her father. "Just?" I remember my spontaneous surprise. I gently encouraged her to go beyond her rationalistic tendencies that resisted taking the imaginative exercise of speaking with her deceased father seriously. Jenni is not alone in this hesitation to engage with "spirits" for fear of being seen as crazy. Hallucinatory events in grief are thought to be quite common, though underreported for exactly that reason: the fear of being seen as irrational. As a scientist, Jenni had an even greater investment than the average American, perhaps, in being seen as "rational." Jenni's self-limiting judgments were subtle but clear. These habits encroached on every aspect of her life, yet we saw her begin to release those restraints. In fact, she had been having a hard time getting pregnant, but by the end of our work together, we all rejoiced when she reported to the group that she and her husband were expecting their first child. In her evaluation of the program, Jenni wrote that the process had helped her get unstuck and make real progress with her grief.

Another member of the group, Dave, to my astonishment, had no trouble engaging with spirits. He regaled us with his encounters with his grandmother's ghost, which he reported had colorfully appeared to him at his bedside. And I must admit, this broke down a stereotype I didn't even know I had—thinking men likely had *more*, not less trouble than women with the notion of encountering spirits. Dave experienced a more typical hallucinatory event often discussed in bereavement literature. He'd encountered an apparition, or actual physical manifestation of the person in an attenuated sense—more ephemeral or insubstantial than a living being would be, but nonetheless, clearly recognizable and visually present.

Before my own familial "visitation," knowing of the possibility of a hallucinatory experience, I specifically "told" my deceased father not to show up visually, as Dave had experienced in relation to his grandmother. I was willing to be visited and welcomed a symbolic or indirect apprehension of my dead father, like Jane's blaring fire alarms, as opposed to some direct physical representation, which I expected would terrify me. All of which is to say that I was impressed that Dave's query was not about history or purgatory, and certainly not about a resistance to apprehension of spirits. His concern was with the biblical basis for notions of heaven and hell.

Raised Roman Catholic, Dave had a vague feeling he might be committing idolatry by trying on these Japanese ritual forms. He'd scoured the Bible for the first few weeks of our group meetings, looking to orient himself with respect to our efforts. He wanted to know if he had permission to do this or not.

I understood his concern over idolatry. I told him how I'd experienced my own fear of engaging in "idol worship" when I had knelt years earlier before a huge lacquer altar to the side of the main worship space in the Buddhist temple in Kyoto. My in-laws and I had gathered there on the anniversary of a family member's death. In hierarchical order, we made our way to this altar one by one to offer incense at the appointed place in the service. As I put my pinch of incense on the burner, I chided myself, "What was I, a baptized and confirmed Christian, doing?" Vague recollections of the prohibitions in the Old Testament against worshipping the foreign gods of foreign peoples disturbed me.

At the earliest opportunity, I'd phoned my father, an Episcopal priest in Michigan. To my amazement, he'd reminded me that I was the foreigner there, and he'd encouraged me to remember that "while in Rome . . . ." I had been flabbergasted.

As I began to research how Americans have encountered these resources to date, I came across the website of a Japanese temple located in the United States. One of the comments an American visitor had left was about just how foreign the whole thing felt—and in that, not inviting, but off-putting. The feeling of "foreignness" is precisely what I was trying, in my pilot project, to find a way to lessen in order to make these resources available to the grieving public.

Dennis Klass, an American therapist and bereavement researcher, whose work I touch on in the next chapter, discovered his patients were spontaneously creating the very same kind of rituals and honoring the "continuing bonds" with their deceased loved ones that the Japanese have conducted and embodied through hōji and kuyō for a very long time. With Fenn's help, I've been able to ratify philosophically, in addition to pragmatically, a hunch I'd had, a hope I'd harbored, that these Japanese rituals were less foreign than we might think. Even before encountering Fenn, I'd come across an old text written by a baron in the late nineteenth century that took to task the way Europeans had castigated the practices that they erroneously dubbed "ancestor worship" by pointing out that it was *veneration*, not "worship," and that it is provided for in the fifth of the Ten Commandments in the Christian tradition: *Honor thy father and thy mother*.[14]

In Fenn's treatment of the aftereffects of the practice and discipline of purgatory, he identified several seminal thinkers on both sides of the pond—Dante, Baxter, Locke, Channing, Dickens, and Emerson—whose writings sounded notes similar to the instructions I'd received from the head abbot at the Tofukuji monastery in Kyoto—Fukushima Keido—about the nature of the Japanese rituals, their purposes, and the proper behavior with respect to them.

I'd met Keido when he gave a lecture at Harvard during an annual visit to some twenty universities in the United States, as the successor to the famous D. T. Suzuki, who had first promulgated Zen in the West two generations earlier. When I approached Keido after the lecture about my research on hōji, he invited me to visit him at his monastery when I was in Kyoto that summer. During that visit, he kindly agreed to be my mentor for the fieldwork I was undertaking for my doctoral dissertation. Fenn's use of the English writers, I was thrilled to realize, showed—by comparison to Keido's teaching—that these rituals, their guiding metaphors, and their existential aims need not remain culturally bound. Like Christian claims across the centuries, there are universals governing these rites available for any inquiring mind and seeking soul.

Changing Conceptions of Heaven and Hell

Fenn observed that not only has purgatory diminished in importance, but also the conceptions of heaven and hell have undergone a change as well. This matters greatly to the bereaved as they attempt to cope with their fear of what has happened to their loved one and where they "go" after death. No wonder Dave had to go looking for an anchor in the Bible to shore up his flagging notions. Dave seemed to have lost his place and initially cast about for mooring in his mourning, much like Ruth, Mariah, Jane, Katie, and others.

Over the first couple of weeks the group met, Dave gave up his quest for orienting himself with the help of biblical references to heaven and hell. He didn't find them, but what he *did* find was a lot more hopefulness in what we were doing and how. And since hope is a key thrust of the gospel narratives, I felt it consistent with the gospel imperative to let his query rest in the discovery of such hope.

It wasn't until much later, on reading Richard Fenn's book *The Persistence of Purgatory*, that I came to understand Dave's quest in light of Fenn's accounts of more recent Anglo-American history. Fenn noted that, in addition to the loss of an overt reckoning through purgatory, we no longer orient ourselves with respect to heaven and hell. He wrote, "It is only with the loss of a vivid cultural imagination regarding heaven and hell that it has become difficult to conceive of souls who have lost their place."[15]

But all is *not* lost, I would argue. Fenn chronicled authors whose primary function was to relocate "heaven and hell" not to some physical realm separated from us by death, as purgatory had devolved to purport, but to the "here and now," which was increasingly understood as a function of the quality of our lives and our consciousness. As with Greenblatt's assessment, so, too, Fenn valorizes the imagination. An imagination can be, of course, a constructive force or a destructive one. Fenn is concerned with the imagination's perversion in paranoia, which he observes in its milder— but perhaps more pernicious and pervasive—form as Charles Dickens's "Universal Distrust."

Universal Distrust

To further answer Katie's question about why we, in the United States, need help now with grief, Fenn finds in Charles Dickens a worthy observer of American life. Two passages from Dickens's *American Notes* explain experiences I've had, as well as other pilot project participants' reports, and his concept of Universal Distrust helps me understand why and how Americans might have eschewed the social support necessary for grieving. In the first passage, Dickens identifies Universal Distrust as a key component of the American psyche and social life.[*,16] It's awfully difficult to *get* social support when you're suspicious of or judgmental about everyone! Writing in the mid-nineteenth century, Dickens attributed this distrust to our growing geographical isolation, which was exacerbated by our westward expansion into forbidding territory, further compounding our sense of being cut off. In addition, Fenn claims that the purgatorial impulse to test *oneself* as part of the hope to spend as little time as possible in purgatory has gone underground and is now expressed in a compulsive, implicit *testing of others*. In other words, although we in the mainline Protestant denominations no longer think about purgatory, the concept still affects us in the form of our testing one another, according to Fenn.

In our current political climate, where each side so profoundly distrusts the other, Fenn's analysis suggests that the origin of this polarization is as old as Henry VIII's banning of the purgatorial schema. Without the imaginative construct of purgatory and its rituals to manage our grief—a place to put it, so to speak, a channel for it—we lack a sufficient structure for ourselves and our fellow survivors and a guide to appropriate conduct with each other. As a result, we settle for superficial engagement with each other or treat one another badly due to displaced emotions: feelings that may

---

* For readers who, as I do, appreciate older diction and the riches it contains, here's Dickens's original phrasing: "One great blemish in the popular mind of America, and the prolific parent of an innumerable brood of evils, is Universal Distrust. Yet the American citizen plumes himself upon this spirit, even when he is sufficiently dispassionate to perceive the ruin it works; and he will often adduce it, in spite of his own reason, as an instance of the great sagacity and acuteness of the people, and their superior shrewdness and independence."

be deflected, denied, or dissociated, and from there, exert an outsized and misdirected force.

My pilot project groups were also rather cautious in the beginning, exhibiting a form of Universal Distrust that Dickens spoke of. I knew something of this, painfully, from being a "cradle Episcopalian"—years of living as one of "God's frozen chosen." But I most pointedly came up against this basic distrust unwittingly in a conversation with my father. It turned out that my father, over the course of getting to know Japan through a few trips there and the good offices of my husband and his family, had become quite enamored of the culture. So much so that, when it came time for us to baptize our son, my father asked me why I would even want to do that. "You've made it out," he stated, somewhat plaintively. "Why would you want to burden the poor child with Christianity?"

Needless to say, this was not what I expected. He'd been adamant about wanting a priestly role in my wedding. And he'd steered me clear of my fear of idolatry in a healthy respect for another culture, an open-mindedness that is consistent with the "broad theology" of Anglican tradition. Although my husband and I hadn't exactly anticipated this response on his part, we were ready for him. If our son were, as the famous British psychoanalyst D. W. Winnicott observed about himself, to outgrow Christianity, we understood we nevertheless needed to provide him with a foundation for that outgrowing.

But then my conversation with my father took an unforeseen turn. I asked some question about baptism, and he gave a textbook answer that I have forgotten. What I do remember is my reply, formed from a culmination of a decade of living in Japan, having had nothing to do with the church during all that time but clearly still thinking in theological terms, if only subliminally. What I said was by way of a mild challenge to his textbook reply: "Doesn't that really depend on just how much you truly believe that anyone and everyone could be the Christ?"

It was his turn to be flabbergasted. I don't recall where the conversation went from there; what I do recall is my own shock and realization of something that had lain dormant for that decade: a sense of my own calling to the priesthood. I understood in a flash that I *trusted*, where my father had never seemed able to do so. I supposed that his distrust accounted for the difficulties he'd had in his ministry.

At that moment, however, I felt as if I stood in a wide-open clearing, breathing freely, whereas before I had been hemmed in and suffocated by his suspiciousness—along with the secondhand smoke from his two-and-a-half packs of Marlboros a day. I'd inhaled for decades my father's distrust, which had crippled me, but during my decade in Japan, I had been breathing in a different air. And I breathed a sigh of relief that, having been graced with a grasp of this fundamental faith, I would possibly be spared my father's mistakes (I was clear, though, that I'd make my own). But I had needed that delineation, that separation between us. I'd needed to find my own stance, my own understanding, the basis for me to live and work and have my being. I'd needed to learn to trust. With that utterance, something was severed between us, and the groundwork was laid for both a security and a freedom to take root within me.*

As I write this, I am aware of a distinction that had previously eluded me. It's not that the Japanese are naively trusting and go about glibly offering support or advice to fellow survivors of a loss, much less unsolicited hugs! That sort of fly-by-night exchange, I maintain, is *far* from what I sense makes hōji and kuyō effective. To the contrary, in interviews with the director of the Oscar-winning Japanese film *Drive My Car*, a profound meditation on the losses suffered by the two main characters, Hamaguchi talked about the long silences in the movie as his attempt to show the protagonists' careful weighing of "not this, not that" as they took the time to try to find the right thing to say to the other, who was grieving.

Rituals attending grief create a context in which reverence is cultivated (more on reverence in chapter 6) over an extended, prolonged period. Different from the one-and-done of Protestant funerals or the occasional

---

* For a liberating understanding of "faith" *not* as assent to dogma, doctrine, or formulae of "beliefs" but rather as *trust*, see Harvey Cox's *The Future of Faith* (HarperOne, 2009).

memorial event, *daily* ablutions make reverence a default disposition. Ironically, even while the Japanese are focused inward during their grief rituals, they also tend to bring that focus outward toward caring for others, and not just in their grief. The best illustration of this for me, while somewhat abstract, is a TV show from the 1980s called *Naruhodo! The World*, or "Ah! I Get You, World!" The program visited another, often exotic or seemingly primitive, society and presented implements that were not easily identifiable. A panel of Japanese people was asked to guess how this implement was used. Their explanations for such objects carried a palpable sense of the panelists' capacity for fellow-feeling, their appreciation for the tasks of daily living, and the effort needed for completing them—demonstrating, one might say, their groundedness. When the purpose of the implement was disclosed, there was always a sense of awe—an important component of reverence—undergirding their appreciation for the ingenuity involved.

I often felt burdened by the enormous bureaucratic apparatus in Japan, the security measures that they took for granted but that we, in the States, are only reluctantly coming to embrace as necessary. But what makes this different from Dickens's notion of Universal Distrust is that, in my experience, the Japanese are still linked with the rest of humankind through an acceptance and *appreciation of* their own humanity—as I've tried to illustrate in my description of the TV show *Naruhodo! The World*. While Japan is certainly as guilty as we are in the West of the ravishes of imperialism, greed and, sadly, sheer sadism, they also embrace many habits of humility that both hone a healthier and more constructive feeling of interdependence as well as embody it. Many people in the United States are developing habits of putting their hands together in a prayerful pose and bowing—athletes, guests on a TV talk show, to name a few ready examples. And collaborative styles of work and study abound. But in general, I believe it's still fair to say that we, in the States, still want to be "unique." We have a "manifest destiny" to lead the rest of the world, to be the light to the nations, to be exceptional. In our hyperindividualized society, each of us must live out our "unique destiny." And worse: as psychologist Rollo

May observed in 1972 (a year before Ernest Becker published his Pulitzer Prize–winning *The Denial of Death*),

> An American receives very little aid from his culture in carrying this [extreme emphasis on individual] responsibility. Americans have no sacraments like penance, no rituals like confession (except in psychoanalysis for the few) to help free them from the burden of the past. The whole weight rests on the shoulders of the individual, and . . . he feels powerless . . . In any case, a person cannot carry the burden of responsibility for his own moral salvation without a corresponding depth of culture to give him structure. Otherwise he will end up feeling isolated, lonely, and separated from others.[17]

My sense is that hōji and kuyō create and sustain the "depth of culture" in Japan that Rollo May notes is necessary, providing contexts for confession and possibilities of penance that offset the ever-present dangers of isolation, loneliness, and separation from others. Of course, this has an important qualifier: This potential of these rites is available when practiced appropriately. And, of course, there's no guarantee of that. What I tried to do in the pilot project and now here again is to offer the guidance necessary to that end as I was taught by the priests of various Buddhist sects and the head abbot of a prominent Zen monastery who had abundant experience supervising their parishioners and novices and in turn oversaw my dissertation research in Japan.

In Japan, by contrast, individuality is assumed and esteemed but does not need to be asserted or fought for; the collective, too, has a place—a place of honor. And within that collective, what matters is *not* "the group," as we in the West have mistakenly assumed for a very long time; rather, it's *relationship* that is of paramount value. Not independence nor dependence, but the oft-touted, though difficult-to-achieve, interdependence. The Japanese have valued and mastered the ability to negotiate one's own *agenda* for the health, safety, or well-being of a relationship or the *relationships within the group*. We do not and have not. And we seem to have a long way to go to get there.

The smug assertion of superiority that Dickens noticed in the United States has always seemed to me a sign of insecurity—an insecurity born of neglecting relationships, I have come to see. This insecurity is fostered by our lack of the skills and tools needed *for* relationship. Dickens observed that "individualism outside the context of community could be destructive."[18] This is a lesson we have yet to learn.

The Absence of Etiquette

The difficulty of learning how to overcome the destructive possibilities of individualism entails another major observation Dickens makes: the absence of etiquette—that which smooths social interaction and anchors support offered to the bereaved in both a respect for the other and a humility about oneself. It prevents the kind of "hug rape" that so hurt and offended Mariah, creating the exact opposite effect from what her well-meaning friends intended. The etiquette embraced in Japan—which I detail more in the next chapter—instead provides for the possibility of a pregnant pause that finds gentler, more appropriate expression. In a more general sense, Fenn quotes Dickens:

> I was quite oppressed by the prevailing seriousness and melancholy air of business: which was so general and unvarying, that at every new town I came to, I seemed to meet the very same people I had left behind me, at the last. Such defects as are perceptible in the national manners, seem, to me, to be referable, in a great degree, to this cause: which has generated a dull, sullen persistence in coarse usages, and rejected the graces of life as undeserving of attention.[19]

I have tremendous sympathy for the demands the early Americans endured in establishing a new life in a deeply hostile environment. Surely, one might become short-tempered in such a situation and normal social graces take a back seat. And, of course, much of the impetus for coming to the New World was a rejection of British class society and what was seen as its pretentious manners, putting on airs.

But there is a middle ground, one that need not accentuate the social distance between individuals, but rather heal the breach. P. M. Forni established the Civility Project at Johns Hopkins to aid America in reconnecting with considerate, empathic styles of relating that have lamentably fallen by the wayside—even though they, too, are part of our collective past. In a group I facilitated after the pilot project, we made much use of Forni's work in helping a woman with cognitive impairment from an accident navigate the demands of her life that resulted from that loss. Together, we worked on simple, graceful, and considerate ways she could communicate with folks who tried to do things *for* her, when all she needed was a bit of time and space to achieve whatever she was doing for herself, by herself. She had been deeply hurt by what she experienced as patronizing condescension. She had been, after all, a very accomplished person, functioning at high levels of cognitive achievement before the accident had caused permanent brain injury. She needed to preserve relationships while asserting her competence and independence. Applying Forni's methods, she started with an empathic disclaimer ("I know and appreciate that you're trying to help"), followed by a gentle assertion ("but I can do this, want to do this, and would like you just to stand by, if you don't mind").

I suspect that greasing the wheels of social intercourse is what Rickie, a member of the second group in my pilot project, found and valued when I explained my love of Japanese forms of etiquette. I often modeled one form by beginning our sessions with the statement the Japanese might use to begin an encounter with anyone they hadn't seen for a bit: "*Senjitsu wa sumimasen deshita*" or "*shitsurei shimashita*" is an acknowledgment that "I may have offended you last time we met and request your forgiveness." I almost wrote "indulgence" in place of "forgiveness" because that is the true sense of the sentiment and expression—that the speaker is begging the indulgence of their friend for whatever might have offended them. And I suspect it *is* an "indulgence" worthy of instituting, as did Rickie. In our final session, she insisted that I include mention of it in this book.

Given the surplus of emotion we feel during bereavement, it makes sense that we fear the damage done to relationships by the honest expression of our emotions. Our American culture lacks an adequate etiquette that seeks to honor the other while presenting oneself with sufficient humility so as not to offend, an etiquette grounded in reverence. Without an etiquette that forms a structured social support for what to say and how to act, a vicious cycle is established: Stifling expression creates distance, then uncontrolled eruptions of too much emotion cause even greater ruptures, which are again stifled, and the cycle begins again. In place of preserving relationships, they are instead increasingly impoverished or impaired, or at the very least, become more distant and shallower. Where depth might be possible, even desirable, a superficial exchange suffices. Sort of. And so, here we are: a coarse culture laced with Universal Distrust, and as Thomas Lynch believes, "ritually adrift, metaphorically impoverished, and existentially vexed."[20] Oh my.

Though we are in pieces at the moment, we, as fragments, are begging to be reunited in a loving, comprehensive whole. And the hints for this bridge building are, gratefully, all around us.

Grief During the Civil War and Since

Like the conversation that Jane, my pilot project participant, had with her fundamentalist son, where the customs we were trying on provided the occasion for bridge building, the Civil War provided the context for a constructive reciprocity between Black and White. American historian and author of *This Republic of Suffering: Death and the American Civil War*, Drew Gilpin Faust, described the efforts of some Blacks in the South who tended Yankee graves as gestures of gratitude, respect, and political assertiveness. Faust cited the patriotic norm of the time: the willingness to give one's life for one's country—then more of a general impulse, not reserved to the enlisted folks or military: "This was a war of mass citizens' armies, not of professional, regular forces; it was a war in which the obligation of the citizen to the nation was expressed as a willingness to risk life itself."[21]

Following on the efforts to relocate heaven and hell in the qualities of life on earth, the picture of "the geography and society" of the afterlife shifted, and the common notion was of an "eternal family reunion" where one would be reunited after death with loved ones. Assuaging the unbearable pain of parting, visions of heavenly reunion proliferated, grounded largely in notions of death not being an ending, per se, but merely a "crossing." Faust writes:

> Earlier visions of heaven had focused almost exclusively on the connection between God and man within the heavenly kingdom, *even to the point of denying the persistence of earthly ties of family and friendship.* But Swedenborg and thinkers influenced by his views created the foundation for what now came to seem a necessary component of an adequately consoling portrait of paradise.[22] (emphasis added)

Faust's historical depiction of that vertical emphasis I had experienced in the first offering at my Japanese altar finally makes sense of my feeling of "things being filled in on a horizontal plane": the persistence of earthly ties of family and friendship. Apparently, along with the rest of Western culture, I'd been good at denying, shoving to the side, or completely dissociating the importance of family and friends. My sense of satisfaction in that early moment in front of my Japanese altar now seems justified by it allowing me to retrieve an essential ingredient in a happy life: an emphasis on relationships.

Amid all the chaos of the Civil War, and in addition to this change in the way heaven was conceived, several other advances also occurred: an improved effort at recordkeeping: counting the dead, informing next of kin. The moral imperative to do so was keenly and universally felt, and the effort soldiers made to send loving last words placed an emphasis on emotion and communication of it, as well as awareness of and preparation for the end that Philippe Ariès, who recognized our inability to talk about death, would commend.

Taken altogether, these responses of our countrymen to the overwhelming nature of death during the Civil War still impress with their community, ethnic, and religious ties—qualities Faust laments we currently lack. This echoes Thomas Lynch's notion of the "changing mythologies of extinction," which have left us unsure, or "vexed" in Lynch's terms. Faust writes:

> We still seek to use our deaths to create meaning where we are not sure any exists. The Civil War generation glimpsed the fear that still defines us—the sense that death is the only end. We still work to live with the riddle that they—the Civil War dead and their survivors alike—had to solve so long ago.[23]

The Civil War provided the context for the recovery of emotion, which had been suppressed through the well-meaning but misguided efforts of Protestant preaching since the ban on purgatory, the communication of which is surely critical in cultivating deep, satisfying, and lasting ties. And now modern times have seen a plethora of approaches for what to do with all that feeling. I'm not persuaded, though, that without the intentional cultivation of reverence and humility that these approaches help with the management of emotion or the establishment of meaningful relationships. In the next chapter, I explore how meaningful relationships are critical both for grieving and a satisfying life more generally.

With Faust's account of the nature of death and bereavement in the Civil War period, we have arrived at the threshold of the more thoroughly modern period, marked so indelibly by the contributions of Sigmund Freud. Freud's *Mourning and Melancholia*, written in 1917, casts a pall (so to speak) over the rest of that century that still affects us in ours.[24] Now we will explore the paths trod by anthropology and psychology as they wended their way through the fissures left by the ban on purgatory in an attempt to fill the cracks created by our lack of ritual means for helping us with our grief.

2

Theory and Therapy

We find psychologists blaming doctors for seeing grief as an
illness, sociologists blaming psychologists for drawing universal
conclusions from the study of one particular culture . . .

—COLIN MURRAY PARKES

n this chapter, I want to continue with my attempt to answer Katie's question about how we got "here," including a fuller description of just where that "here" is. In the previous chapter, I outlined the history of the West's troubled relationship with mourning rituals, which revolved around notions of purgatory since the eleventh century. Then the idea of purgatory fell subject to abuse and was banned by Henry VIII of England. With America's roots in British history, the dominant culture in the United States has yet to see any religious rites rise to the prominence of purgatorial practices, though there are subcultures—Jewish, Catholic, Latinx, and others—whose mourning observances arguably provide more social support and ritual resources than are available in mainline Protestant Christian denominations. Most of the rest of us remain, though, as undertaker Thomas Lynch lamented, "ritually adrift, metaphorically impoverished and existentially vexed."

I want to paint the picture of what has arisen in place of ritual and religious resources as a potpourri of psychological theory of—if not practices for—bereavement. For suggestions on how to "do" bereavement better, this brief history will involve a look at the anthropology of grief as well, focusing on how anthropology and psychology approached the topic of grief from different angles.

The Continuing Misapplication of the Five Stages

Most people have heard of the five stages of grief. But not everyone is aware, including my well-educated and articulate friend Gordon, of the tremendous amount of ink spilled recently in certain circles debunking the stages established in the late 1960s by Dr. Elisabeth Kübler-Ross. I sat next to Gordon at dinner the night before a memorial service for his parents. Gordon thoughtfully remarked that, as he observed his own process, he found the stages (denial, anger, bargaining, depression, and acceptance) just didn't seem to fit him. I was impressed with his emotional sensitivity, intellectual courage, and integrity in going against the grain, since the five stages remain a large part of the grieving guidance groundwater in the United States. For a fascinating account of just how thoroughly saturated we are in stage theory, you might find journalist Ruth Davis Konigsberg's account in *The Truth About Grief: The Myth of Its Five Stages and the New Science of Grief* a helpful resource and interesting read.[1] It is also noteworthy that, though from a distinguished family of ministers and himself a religion scholar, Gordon turned to a psychological resource in his grief. A powerful testament to the scarcity of resources within today's leading religious denominations and the ways psychological sources have attempted to fill the gap.

Happily, it didn't seem that Gordon was complaining that anyone *else* had tried to pigeonhole him into one of the stages. Trying to work with an unworkable model on one's own can be bad enough. I mention this because Wesley Carr, former dean of Westminster Abbey, liturgist for Princess Diana's funeral, and author of the slim volume *Brief Encounters: Pastoral*

Ministry Through Baptisms, Weddings and Funerals, presciently observed way back in 1985 that clergy did more harm than good by trying to pinpoint the stage a parishioner was "in," rather than listen open-mindedly and large-heartedly to what that person might be saying to him or her.[2] As we saw in Stephen Greenblatt's thorough examination of what has become of grieving since the loss of the purgatorial scheme, Anglican clergy were prone to admonish their flock to stoicism and even cheerfulness as the attitude appropriate for inheritors of eternal life, as believers were believed to be. I think of it as a "rush to the resurrection."*

Nicholas Peter Harvey, a compatriot of Carr's, wrote *Death's Gift: Chapters on Resurrection & Bereavement* to slow things down and remind readers that even the disciples had to undergo a period of waiting after Jesus's resurrection: an agonizing period of fifty days, at the end of which they finally experienced the comfort attributed to Christ's sending of the Holy Spirit to them in what is now celebrated and commemorated as the Feast of Pentecost.[3] This period, incidentally, corresponds almost exactly with the first official period of mourning in Japan observed in the rites I am commending, marked and ended by a public ritual on the forty-ninth day. But I'm getting ahead of myself.

HuffPost recently published a simpler, straightforward critique of the five stages of grief, with special mention of how—in keeping with Carr's concern with a "rush to the resurrection"—the stages have become something of a contest to get through. Acknowledging that Kübler-Ross herself lamented the misuse her work had been put to, Megan Devine, author of "The Five Stages of Grief and Other Lies That Don't Help Anyone," states: "They [the five stages] are firmly embedded in our cultural ideas of the right and wrong ways to grieve. The stages are used as a corrective reproach, the process of grief turned into a race."[4]

No wonder Mariah was afraid she'd gotten it wrong.

---

* I thought Wesley Carr coined this phrase, but I haven't been able to find it in his *Brief Encounters: Pastoral Ministry Through Baptisms, Weddings and Funerals* (SPCK Publishing, 1994). It may be an instance in which I myself coined this phrase as an easy-to-remember gloss on his work. I seem to do that! If you come across his using this phrase, please let me know!

Recently, I came across a website, What's Your Grief?, established by two mental health workers in the Baltimore area, who colorfully and in simple language present a host of articles to help individual grievers, including a whole section on many of the same theorists I will talk about here.

So, while it's become something of a cottage industry lately to debunk Kübler-Ross (K-R) and try on alternatives, I see the vehemence of protests around the misuse of her stages—which were, in actuality, about the process the *dying* go through in coming to terms with their *own* death, not the survivors attempting to deal with the death of a loved one—as part of the frustration we have in this culture with finding anything adequate to replace them: structure, support, and guidance for our grieving. The What's Your Grief? website provides an opportunity for visitors to leave feedback, and many have expressed profound gratitude for the website, especially for mention of the "continuing bonds" theory, which I'll get to in a moment.[5] But in spite of all these individual testimonials and earnest expressions of gratitude, one commenter lamented our culture's lack of both the time and the space for grief. Aye, there's the rub! While it's now commonplace that grieving takes time and, at least, in some instances, may never end, we have yet to figure out how to provide the kind of space that is good—a constructive context—for grief. And this is the gap I am trying to address.

But before I go much further, I should acknowledge that, while one of my pilot project participants had sought out other grief support approaches, none came to my project professing a specific dissatisfaction with the Kübler-Ross schema. The pilot project participants were, however, to a person, aware that they had suffered a loss that they felt had been insufficiently attended to; and they were willing—and eager—to explore a resource from abroad to address this lack.

Ambivalence and Taking the Time to Grieve

For a better appreciation of where we are now and how we've landed here, I want to take a moment to understand what K-R was trying to do—as well as why. Kübler-Ross was the most prominent among a few American psychologists who tried their hand at operationalizing the vague imperative that Freud issued to do grief work in his monumental *Mourning and Melancholia*, published in 1917.[6] Freud's purpose in that essay was, unfortunately for us, *not* to delineate what comprised healthy grief, much less how to go about it, but to delineate how it could go wrong and end up in a stagnant state he called "melancholia." Here, I believe, is a deeper antecedent to Mariah's fear of not doing it right, and a source of Ruth's need for a "how-to" to begin with, as well as the impetus for my intrepid twelve to join me in my pilot project.

"Melancholia," according to Freud, is a result of ambivalent feelings toward the deceased, specifically of the repressed sort, which, going undetected, exert a mysterious and pervasively dampening effect on the whole personality. Unable to experience and "resolve" those ambivalent feelings and therefore safely and completely withdraw one's interest in the deceased, one didn't have the emotional energy or, more generally, the life force (what he called "libido," since everything to Freud was sexual) to reinvest in relationships with the living. So Freud's theory goes. Until recently, therapy for the bereaved since the time of Freud revolved around making conscious the repressed ambivalence toward the deceased that was thought to be standing in the way of a healthy "resolution" of or "recovery" from one's grief. In Freud's reckoning, "resolving" one's grief takes time.

I have long had a hunch that Freud got this idea—of grief taking time— from the work of anthropologist Robert Hertz. Hertz's landmark essay "A Contribution to the Study of the Collective Representation of Death" was published in 1907—ten years before Freud's *Mourning and Melancholia*.[7] Hertz described his discovery of secondary burial customs in rural France. A few years after the initial burial, the community would gather to dig up the remains of the deceased. Then they would rebury them. Hertz posited that this was to assist in their coming to terms—psychologically or emotionally—with the fact of the death, as it was too overwhelming at first to take it all in. I was impressed with Hertz's sensitive and imaginative empathizing, which led him to this conclusion.

Peter Gay, in his sample volume of Freud's writings, does acknowledge that Freud was an avid reader of anthropology.[8] So it isn't far-fetched to suppose that Freud may have lifted the idea of grieving over time from Hertz's essay. In any event, it seemed from that time forward, psychology and anthropology pursued a kind of division of labor, psychology tending to the inner world, anthropology documenting externals like kinship structures, the form that rituals took, and the like.

I was, frankly, a bit distressed at this fragmentation and wondered if ever the twain would meet. I was especially disheartened to read Evans-Pritchard, a British anthropologist half a century later, in the 1960s, denounce Hertz's emotional interpretation as "unfounded."[9]

It was at the Evans-Pritchard point—the 1960s, half a century since Freud—that K-R came on the scene. Erich Lindemann, a German psychiatrist steeped in analytical training, had made an earlier attempt to study and describe grief.[10] The Cocoanut Grove fire of 1942, a nightclub inferno in Boston, Massachusetts, in which 492 people perished, served as the impetus to expand on his earlier studies of the grief that only entailed the loss of a limb or other body part. Lindemann documented—through extensive interviews with the more than three hundred survivors of the fire—patterns of response to the disaster, including somatic distress (trouble sleeping, eating, and worse); hostility; anger; identifying with the deceased and, in particular, trying to live out the ideals they embraced; and finally, a preoccupation with the deceased, including various hallucinatory experiences.

Building on his earlier work, Lindemann registered an important criterion for what and why we grieve some things or people and not others: We grieve the loss of people who are an important part of our *social* world, noting that such losses feel like losing a part of ourselves. Absent control groups in the study of the Cocoanut Grove fire, his research more closely approximated the methods of anthropological fieldwork. And, in fact, differently from how Freud focused on unconscious processes as a key to unlocking the truth about humanity, Lindemann's angle concerned the social nature and effects of grief. His method combined insights from psychology, anthropology, and ethology. Among his chief discoveries was how recovery for soldiers, during war, was greatly facilitated by their recuperation *on the battlefield*, instead of removing them from the theater of war and their comrades. In contrast to Freud's insistence on getting at the unconscious ambivalence of survivors of a loss, Lindemann was keen on reconnecting the bereaved with their social world.

A recent article in *The Harvard Crimson* noted about Lindemann's work that "this is impossible without the *cooperation* of the living world. Recovery, then, would require the *whole community*" (emphasis added) in a competent, cooperative, and supportive role—not in denial, dismissal, or toxic positivity.[11] Indeed, Lindemann himself notes that some people can be "pathogenic agents"! So not only does it make sense that Mariah and Ruth reached out to me, but it doubly makes sense that Sunny, Mariah's sidekick, was eager to find a way to be part of that whole community and cooperate with—rather than inhibit, frustrate, or compound—Mariah's grief.

The difficulty we've had in incorporating these insights into our grieving practices to date might well be attributed, in part, to the resistance in the medical field itself to Lindemann's method and insights, along with our outsized reliance on the medical profession in dealing with our grief, *minus* these understandings. In 1954, Lindemann became chief of psychiatry at Mass General and a professor of psychiatry at Harvard Medical School. But one of his students in the 1950s and '60s, Charles G. Satin, reflected on the resentment Lindemann eventually encountered. "And when he involved non-medical people in psychology, anthropology, sociology . . . the medical people were just outraged—letting all these non-medical people into our citadel, and polluting the purity of medicine."[12]

It was into this rarefied atmosphere that Elisabeth Kübler-Ross came to the United States from her native Switzerland to continue her training as a psychiatric resident in 1958. Her dismay at the medical establishment and, in particular, the brusque way doctors were treating terminally ill patients led her to do a series of interviews with those patients in the hopes of providing better training for physicians in dealing with them. This led to her book *On Death and Dying*, published in 1969, where she expounded on the five stages of grief.[13]

Like Lindemann, K-R was also critical of the way psychiatry generally went about its business, and in the late 1970s, she, too, attempted to integrate other areas of inquiry, taking an interest in spiritualism, near-death experiences, and communicating with the dead. Unfortunately, as a sad commentary on the trend of seeking clairvoyants that Fenn bemoaned and I discussed in chapter 1, she was duped by a man claiming to channel spirits, which ended in scandal.

The Denial of Death and Its Destructiveness

These two failed attempts in the United States at a rapprochement between psychology and anthropology and other allied fields culminated in Ernest Becker's Pulitzer Prize–winning *The Denial of Death*, published just after his death in 1973.[14] In his book, Becker asserts that our denial had become so pervasive that it represented a veritable cultural disease. In his estimation, it takes more of a toll on us collectively than the combined repressions around sexuality and aggression that Freud bemoaned so heartily. In the late '60s and early '70s, these were fighting words! Becker lambasts a culture of misguided "heroism" as our collective failed attempt to manage the terror of death and dying.

I could relate. It was around this time that my father had open-heart surgery. Not knowing of Becker's work at the time, I thought I was alone in being revolted at the implicit elevation of medicine to a cult-like entity with doctors the high priests emblematized by the "step-down" room where my father would go to recover from the anesthesia post-op, seeming to suggest he'd been on the "high altar" of the surgical table, the sacrificial lamb to the doctor's ego-based heroism. Don't get me wrong: I was and remain deeply grateful that this surgery enabled my father to live another couple of decades. But this should not obscure the nature of the *system* and how it grew to be what it was, and what the cost to society is and was as a result.

Becker writes, "Modern man is drinking and drugging himself out of awareness, or he spends his time shopping, which is the same thing."[15] As an alternative to the ego-driven heroics that our fear of dying demands but our culture no longer provides for (remember, he's writing during the Vietnam era, where support for our troops was at an all-time low), he suggests: "The most that any one of us can seem to do is to fashion something—an object or ourselves—and drop it into the confusion, make an offering of it, so to speak, to the life force."[15]

It would be yet another decade or two after Becker's and K-R's work before a team of eminent researchers headed by Marian Osterweis—who studied bereavement in North America in the 1980s[17]—recommended the very thing that the medical establishment had long eschewed: looking to other cultures ("who do bereavement better") in longitudinal, family-based, prospective, cross-cultural studies to cull practices · for bereavement that could help us in the West do it better.[18]

Psychiatrist and medical anthropologist Arthur Kleinman was a participant in the Osterweis study and joined the group of psychiatrists critical of the medical establishment. His perceptive critique of the practice of medicine for failing to take into account the social world of the patient is *The Illness Narratives*, published in 1988.[19]

It would be almost another decade before I landed on Arthur's doorstep, hoping to do the very thing that he, as part of the team of Osterweis investigators, had recommended—look to other cultures for better methods of bereavement. I had earned my Master of Divinity at Harvard and was embarking on my next step in the doctoral program to study Japanese bereavement customs, with which I'd become thoroughly familiar after marrying into the culture. I was deeply gratified by Arthur's immediate support and enthusiasm. He hastened to express his concern over the current state of his professional guidelines embodied in the fourth edition of the *Diagnostic and Statistical Manual* (DSM-IV), allowing for only two months of somatic distress and other symptoms of bereavement before being deemed "pathological" or "complicated" and requiring or recommending therapy.

He charged me with the task of trying to do a better job of delineating the line between healthy and pathological grief as the key struggle within the area of bereavement at the time. As for method, he advised me to listen open-mindedly, with no preconceptions, to the subjects I would encounter as I did fieldwork in Japan to understand the rituals I am commending here: kuyō and hōji. Ethnography was the mode: being a participant/observer and, through that up-close-and-personal encounter, describing the world under study elaborately, and in fine detail, what is known in anthropology as a thick way.

Grief as a Medical Condition

While labeling grief as "pathological" or "complicated" may have enabled some folks to receive therapy paid for by insurance, it did little for the vast majority of folks who would not seek treatment through medical channels for bereavement. Worse, it seemed to imply to many folks that bereavement *itself* was a "medical condition," not the normal course of things in the wake of loss. And, of course, with few exceptions, bereavement was seen as an *individual* syndrome, to be treated *individually*. And to this doubling down on the hyperindividualism of our current culture, some bereavement specialists and authors have offered the highly individualistic, self-reliant "resilience" as the antidote to the now passé but similarly hyperindividualistic emphasis on "recovery."

In fact, after decades of dedicated research on bereavement—early on, he participated in the Harvard Bereavement Study in the 1960s and later, worked mainly through the Tavistock Institute in London—eminent British psychiatrist Colin Murray Parkes concluded that most people don't need therapy to deal with their grief.[20] He helped discern and address the needs of individuals he and fellow researchers identified as "high-risk" and went on to establish a nationwide volunteer organization in Britain known as Cruse Bereavement Care. They dispatch trained volunteers to the homes of those at risk following a major loss. Parkes partnered with John Bowlby, the originator of attachment theory, a hugely influential departure from Freudian preoccupations that examine how infants bond with their primary caregivers in ways that can be problematic in later life. Parkes and Bowlby discerned their own basic (read: normal) grief schema: numbness and disorientation, yearning and pining, disorganization and reorganization. Parkes makes no bones about the fact that it was controversial. But it was a starting point.[21] They built on that by applying attachment theory to bereavement, trying to discern whether early patterns of relating affected one's ability to cope with later losses in life, in particular.

But Parkes is quick to point out that

> Cross-cultural differences are . . . very great and need to be studied if we are to learn how to mitigate some of the suffering caused by grief. It may well be that certain types of reaction to bereavement are "normal" within certain subcultures and "abnormal" in others, but we should not assume that it follows that what is "normal" is necessarily right, healthy, or harmless.[22]

Getting Beyond the Limitations of the Western Mindset

In a resounding affirmation of Parkes's observation about the need to get outside a particular cultural bias in order to be free to garner the best knowledge, a fascinating article comparing infant attachment styles in the United States and Japan states, "When most investigators [have] . . . a common cultural perspective or ideological position, the effect may be to retard or to corrupt the search for scientific knowledge by collectively blinding them to alternative conceptions."[23]

The authors of that study found that, while a similar distribution of *the types* of attachment may be found in Japan, the essential *character* of attachment itself is quite different. Whereas in the West, infants who are thought to be "securely attached" exhibit exploratory behavior and a readiness to play alone when the parent leaves their infant in a room with a stranger, in Japan, the focus of attachment is helping the child learn behaviors that enhance the child's ability to give and take in appropriate ways and to have relationships of reciprocal care and attentiveness. The article notes that mothers typically never leave their infants alone until they are at least one year old, so "exploratory behavior" and independent play are neither primarily valued nor commonly exhibited as such. While it may be tempting to see this through the usual Western category of "group" versus "individual," "dependence" versus "independence," I want to pause and take a closer look beyond these stultifying stereotypes, lest we miss a critical difference that could be life enhancing for us, should we choose to learn from it.

A book by an early critic of Freud, Ian Suttie, helps ground our appreciation for the difference through a clearer, more constructive lens. Published in 1935, the same week that Suttie died, *The Origins of Love and Hate* outlines Suttie's thesis that our basic drive as human beings is *not* sexual or aggressive, as Freud would have us believe, but *social*. And the basic skill needed for successful social life is the capacity for give-and-take, or, in a word, reciprocity. In his introduction to Suttie's book, Ashley Montagu summarizes: "Where the cornerstone of the Freudian system is 'sex,' in Suttie's it is 'love.' Where Freud speaks of 'libido,' Suttie speaks of 'the need for companionship.'"[24]

This sounds strikingly similar to Lindemann's earliest findings about grief—indeed, it underscores them. Grief entails reconnecting the bereaved with his or her *social* world—and, in doing so, requires the cooperation of the whole community. Suttie seemed to provide a grounding for the specific case of bereavement in a more widespread phenomenon: human nature in general.

So our hyperindividualistic tendencies are really an aberration, a deviation from what we really need and crave. Johann Hari hypothesizes about early humanity in his book *Lost Connections*. Hari notes our origins on the savannah and the highly social nature of that lifestyle. To be alone was to court death, and so the earliest people, he reasons, were motivated to limit anti- or asocial behavior, so as not to be ostracized and left alone.

Now, Hari asserts, because of all our isolating tendencies, "We have been left alone on a savannah we do not understand, puzzled by our own sadness."[25]

If I'd been concerned with the chasm between psychology and anthropology and the impoverishment of our understanding and resources that resulted, Parkes, for his part, was aghast at the fragmentation and antagonisms within the field of bereavement research. He wrote,

> We find psychologists blaming doctors for seeing grief as an illness, sociologists blaming psychologists for drawing universal conclusions from the study of one particular culture, psychiatrists blaming physicians for ignoring the psyche, and ethologists accusing all the rest of anthropocentrism.[26]

In the vacuum created by these struggles, the average mourner is left to his or her own devices. Whatever happened to Lindemann's most fundamental insight, that grieving requires a community for getting it right? Where is that community to be found? And how can that community be cultivated to cooperate?

Remember Sunny, Mariah's friend, who wanted to know how to support Mariah in the wake of her sister's death? Sunny had the right impulse, the right idea: to be a part of the community Mariah needed. But how? Sunny's plight is different, to be sure, than Mariah's own, but that shouldn't tempt us to underrate it. Sunny's desire is itself very basic: the need to give (or is it to respond? Or both?). A desire to do something—something constructive—but clueless about what that entails. Given the ways anthropologists and psychologists have documented the various destructive paths for communal methods of grieving (a Philippine tribe went headhunting and came back with a severed head from a distant tribe; the German penchant for manic economic productivity that generated ire in the United States for its "dumping" practices in the 1960s),[27] Sunny's anxiety itself may not have been misplaced!

Early Grief Support Groups and Creating Community

As Parkes points out, support groups for the recently bereaved are a kind of community and have been a mainstay of grieving help since the late 1960s, when the late psychologist Phyllis Silverman began her renowned "widow-to-widow" program. And yet, these too were ad hoc, ex post facto, task-oriented, and soon disbanded. In a word, more of the fragmentation endemic in our society at present. One of my pilot project participants sampled an ad hoc bereavement program but was dissatisfied with what she called its "gimmick-iness." I myself was taken aback when I visited Phyllis Silverman's brainchild, a house she'd converted into a therapy space for children called, appropri-ately enough, The Children's Room. Phyllis had a lot of good sense about grief, a great deal of experience with it, and had helped many cope. It seemed to me, though, that she was missing an opportunity in some of the games she had the children play, which appeared to be based on an old-school notion that simply "expressing" things about the deceased was a means of mourning them. "What was his favorite color?" was a square on a ball that the chil-dren would toss to each other to take turns expressing something about their loved one who'd died. Over lunch, her penetrating questions about my own work allowed me to mention the possibility of using these sessions with bereaved children to cultivate compassion, not simply regurgitate known things with no import or direction. Sometime after this encounter, I went to The Children's Room website and was encouraged to note that their mission now includes growing in compassion as part of their endeavor.

I haven't been back to see just how they do that. But in my own sup-port groups, as I mentioned in chapter 1, I had a few basic rules and a few guiding principles that were geared toward cultivating compassion and limiting derailment:

- Stick to "*I*-statements."
- Refrain from judgment (of yourself or anyone else's offerings).
- Remember to respect the confidentiality of the group.
- Ask questions to understand better.
- Do "reality-testing" to learn how one's comments or offerings "landed."
- Offer an apology for remarks that went astray and did more harm than good.

Since then, I've also learned a lot more about expressing emotion and the kinds of misunderstandings we might be harboring about it. In Suttie's critique of Freud, he discusses Freud's notion of "detensioning" that results from the expression of emotion. And I can't help but wonder if many of us aren't still affected by erroneous ideas and misleading practices that those ideas generated. For example, therapists in the '80s would often prescribe hitting pillows as a way of dealing with pent-up anger or rage. It was presumably a kind of naïve and hyperindividualistic method for catharsis, but it did not substantially affect either the interpersonal relationship *or* the experience of individuals.

"Offering" in Place of "Expressing"

Suttie addresses my concern over the emphasis on "expression" in our culture when he writes that

> The Freudian conception of self-expression as a "detensioning" process or emotional evacuation now seemed to me false and in its place I imagined expression as an offering or stimulus directed to the other person, designed to elicit a response while love itself was essentially a state of active harmonious interplay.[28]

I love the notion of self-expression as *an offering*, and as essentially *relational*, hallowing it as befitting a *reverential* appreciation of each other and the sacredness of life, work, and play. In other words, self-expression is best experienced *in* relationship, potentially to ameliorate or heal it, as opposed to being an act of one-sided self-indulgence with its aim simply to reduce one's own tension and, bordering on selfishness, potentially increasing one's loneliness and isolation. Understanding our acts of self-expression as offerings sets the stage, I believe, for understanding the role of memorial customs that include ritual offerings and a give-and-take that spans the generations.

Given the "force" of emotion that anthropologist Renato Rosaldo observed and the "surplus" of emotion that German psychoanalysts Alexander and Margarete Mitscherlich noted as characterizing bereavement, the expression of emotion as an offering may seem a stretch. Or, at the very least, require a great deal of discipline. How *can* the feelings that accompany bereavement best be handled? No wonder Ruth needs know-how, Mariah is afraid of doing it wrong, and her sidekick Sunny is similarly at a loss over how to help her friend with her grief. Not to mention Gordon, who found the five steps unhelpful, and Dave, whose early religious training hamstrung him with fear.

In our hyperindividualized culture and moment, the idea of discipline may seem anathema to many. But perhaps that discipline will not seem so oppressive if we understand that we are not being *prevented* from the "detensioning" that Freud made us feel entitled to or was ultimately required for our sanity. To the contrary, I'm hoping that Suttie's insights about an offering will be for you, as they were for me, a respite and relief, a recognition of our natural impulses and desires, a proper acknowledgment of deep, possibly unmet longings. But we may need to borrow an insight from Ruth Benedict, anthropologist and author of *The Chrysanthemum and the Sword*, on the nature of discipline in Japan. She makes it seem almost palatable:

> Americans, in order to understand ordinary self-disciplinary practices in Japan, therefore, have to do a kind of surgical operation on our idea of "self-discipline." We have to cut away the

accretions of "self-sacrifice" and "frustration" that have clustered around the concept in our culture. In Japan one disciplines oneself to be a good player, and the Japanese attitude is that one undergoes the training with no more consciousness of sacrifice than a man who plays bridge. Of course the training is strict, but that is inherent in the nature of things. The young child is born happy but without the capacity to "savor life." Only through mental training (or self-discipline; *shuyo*) can a man or woman gain the power to live fully and to "get the taste" of life. The phrase is usually translated "only so can he enjoy life." Self-discipline "builds up the belly (the seat of control)"; it enlarges life.[29]

She goes on to observe: It's not that the actual frustrations required by such discipline don't take a toll; they well might (as in stomach ulcers and "excessive bodily tensions"):

> But the sanction of reciprocity, and the Japanese conviction that self-discipline is *to one's own advantage*, make many acts seem easy to them which seem insupportable to Americans. They pay much closer attention to *behaving competently* and they allow themselves fewer alibis than Americans. They do not so often project their dissatisfactions with life upon scapegoats, and they do not so often indulge in self-pity because they have somehow or other not got what Americans call average happiness.[30] (emphasis added)

More on Etiquette: Handling the Inadvertent Sins

Rickie, a member of my second group of the pilot project, was adamant in her evaluation that I should mention in this book a form of etiquette, the public expression of the self-discipline Ruth Benedict extols, that I had modeled for them rather compulsively and explained rather effusively.

It had become ingrained in me, having lived in Japan for a decade and speaking the language, to greet someone in the typical way: "*Senjitsu wa sumimasen deshita!*" A loose translation is, "Forgive me for any transgressions I committed the other day!" Literally rendered, it might read as, "I was incomplete the other day!" Or, "What I did the other day was incomplete or inexcusable!" I prefer the first interpretation, giving words to—an interactive acknowledgment of—the "inadvertent sins" we commit. These are the hardest to handle, since often not only are they inadvertent, but we're not even aware that we are committing them. This expression presciently provides a remedy. And while it might be criticized as "pro forma" much of the time in Japan, it still performs a vital function: a humble recognition of the frailty of human interaction and the need for social forms that soothe and smooth.

As I've considered Rickie's insistence, I've wondered how this would be received by my readers. I often found myself musing, "If we can enjoy sushi and sake and say '*sukoshi*,'* surely we can embrace '*Senjitsu wa . . .*' or maybe a less cumbersome and abbreviated version, '*Sumimasen*.'" I often think of a key notion in the Confucian classic, the *I Ching*, as: "Arrogance brings dislike in its train, modesty wins love."[31] This little piece of etiquette, a critical part of Japanese self-discipline, aims at cultivating that humility. What I've come to think of as simply one in a plethora of healthy, helpful "habits of humility."

In that same group of pilot project participants was another member who had a traumatic experience related to being a scapegoat due to others' lack of self-discipline. In grieving, there will be times when one is particularly vulnerable, and immature or unaware folks can take advantage of that vulnerability—like water flowing to the lowest point—to ease their own negative emotions by projecting them outward and making the *other* suffer for what is their own shortcoming. A socially supportive environment, however, can give the bereaved a place to do some reality testing: Is it me, or him? The group provided that context for Carrie, whose boss had

---

* Some readers may have heard the abbreviated form: *sukosh.*

taken advantage of her temporary, grief-induced weakness and mercilessly scapegoated her for a failure of his own. And hōji—if mindfully embraced and executed—can provide the mourner with opportunities for reality testing and support against toxic experiences.

I am not the only American to notice the efficacy of the Japanese memorial rites I am commending. In fact, it was in groups of bereaved American parents that Dennis Klass, a leading bereavement researcher and facilitator—like my friend Gordon with respect to his feelings about his parents—had his own experience of the data not fitting the paradigm. In Klass's case, though, the paradigm wasn't K-R's. He had trained with her before leaving parish ministry and, coached in the ethnographic method by his wife, began simply listening to what the parents had to say. It was much later that he, in one of what he calls "fortuitous events," learned from his son, who was studying in Japan, of the Japanese notion he (or rather, his wife) ended up coining as "continuing bonds." In Klass's assessment, the bereaved parents he was listening to in the grief support groups he facilitated defied the Freudian admonition to cut ties with the deceased in order to return fully to life among the living. Not only did they continue to hold their dead children dear, but they spontaneously created rituals that seemed uncannily like the ones the Japanese have performed for centuries. This is significant as evidence that Americans gravitated toward these sorts of rituals without any instruction at all.

Visitors to the What's Your Grief? website extol in particular the "continuing bonds" notion that the website explains. The curators of the site respond that blogging about their continuing bonds amid their grieving may help to spread the idea and be similarly liberating to others.

This book is my attempt to contribute to that liberation.

While I read Dennis Klass's work as largely descriptive with the hope of being implicitly *prescriptive*, I do in the chapters ahead offer unabashedly prescriptive, hopefully ample description as to how best to go about conducting the rites at the center of my research and recommendation. In place of the commonly held notions about bereavement in which "recovery" is the goal or that "resilience" is the key component, I aim at cultivating reverence as the more adequate framework for including *all* of the prior work in bereavement both here and abroad that hopes for recovery, resolution, and resilience. Reverence allows not only for the time that grieving takes but also for the possibility that it never ends.

The "space and time" that I have experienced Japanese memorial customs encompass will hopefully provide a facilitating environment for the kinds of ideas other workers in the bereavement field have found helpful or even requisite and that I have yet to touch on: Bob Neimeyer's sensitive "meaning-making" approach is one. In case studies of talking with the bereaved, Neimeyer has modeled a vocabulary and stamina essential for probing the experience that helps the survivor ascribe meaning to their loved one's life and death, and in that "meaning-making," find peace with that person's passing.[32] The Europeans Schut and Stroebe describe the "oscillation" entailed in grieving: between a "remembrance" orientation—the emotional work of grief and culling memories to keep—and the "restoration" orientation—creating a new social identity and place for both oneself and the deceased.[33] It provides a sensible pace and reasonable structure for the "tasks" of grieving that psychologist J. W. Worden suggests: 1) accept the reality of the loss; 2) process the pain of grief; 3) adjust to a world without the deceased; and 4) find an enduring connection with the deceased in the midst of embarking on a new life.[34] Japanese memorial customs also have a built-in method for an "apprenticeship in grief" that Francis Weller recommends as an alternative to the "anesthesia and amnesia" that currently take the place of a healthy grief process.[35]

Japanese ritual resources provide the space and time for remembrance in lieu of revenge, as Stephen Greenblatt in the previous chapter told us has been the mandate since the time of Hamlet. And in case Bob Neimeyer's delicate and sensitive search for meaning fails to yield a decisive understanding to ascribe to a death, reverence cultivated through Japanese ritual life can not only supply many more workers for the task of meaning-making in the form of fellow ritual participants, but also promise an ongoing search that need not be sown up within any prescribed time frame. I suspect that

Japanese ritual life in the form of hōji and kuyō, contributes massively to their capacity for—and, indeed, embrace of—uncertainty and ambivalence, qualities that endow their literature with a particular and cherished ambiance too. Most of all, Japanese ritual resources provide *social* opportunities for the kind of support grieving really requires for learning the give-and-take, the reciprocity and discipline needed for being competent in relationship even in the face of death and in that, free to savor life more fully. Granted, this doesn't happen automatically, and a proper understanding of and implementation of the rites is not universal in Japan, just as a proper embrace of any spiritual tradition takes discipline and guidance. I hope to provide some of that guidance—with the help of the pilot project participants' experience and questions—in the next several chapters.

3

The Japanese Rites:
A Primer on Form

nto the breach I went—the breach created in the West's bereavement aids by the historical banning of the purgatorial scheme, compounded by the failure of mainline denominations in the United States to come up with an alternative to facilitate grief, and confounded by the flailing, unavailing attempts of psychology in the West to take up the slack. It was into this chasm I embarked, way back in the mid-1980s, willy-nilly, on my own intrepid venture in experimenting with heretofore unknown—read: foreign—resources.

My little private ritual for my mother's stillborn sister—which I conducted in 1985, at the time my son was born, and described in chapter 1—was a bit like the distilled essence of a larger, public rite. Perhaps like a detailed insert of a portion of a larger map: a close-up of a city and its individual roads in the corner of a big regional map.

During my then three-year-old marriage, I attended many of the large, elaborate, semipublic rituals that my father-in-law held in honor and memory of a host of his deceased relatives. In each one, there was a time for individual attendees to offer their own pinch of incense and to bow in prayer. Tragically, our family had more than most such occasions, in part because my father-in-law had bad luck with wives, who kept predeceasing him. His fourth wife finally outlived him.

In fact, my husband's and my engagement was announced at the first-year memorial event for the second wife, who had opposed our marriage. The timing was a bit too much "over her dead body" for my taste, but I didn't say anything about how macabre that all seemed to me until much later. Later, I was assured it was not an intentional slight or bizarre happening: This is what the Japanese do. They conduct a lot of family business at these ritual occasions because it is the one time that family can be counted on to show up.

Two interwoven factors aid ample attendance, as I learned during my fieldwork in Japan in the early 2000s, then twenty years into our marriage. We'd moved to the States for me to do graduate work, and I was conducting research for my doctoral dissertation. First, there is a schedule of memorial events that extends over time ad infinitum. Second, the schedule itself is a syncopated rhythm that doesn't require memorial events every year: on the contrary.

A Savvy Schedule of Grieving

The syncopated rhythm of hōji entails yearly observances or memorial events for the first two years after a loved one's death, but then the schedule of events begins to skip years in odd intervals: there are public observances—hōji—marking the seventh year, the thirteenth year, the seventeenth year, the twenty-fifth year, the thirty-third year, and the fiftieth year, and then every fifty years thereafter.* Some sects have observances in

---

* Technically, I should probably write "called the seventh year . . . but which actually take place in the sixth year, the twelfth year, and so on." There's a fascinating reason for this: The Japanese start counting matters pertaining to death *before* the event, so let's say the day before or the year before; whereas, in matters of life, like a birthday, years are counted *after* the event: So one is one year old *after* one has lived the first year. My hunch is that this derives from a rather primitive "contagion theory," which is to say, care is taken not to be polluted by contact with the dead, and making sure counters steer clear of creating such contact is one way this is accomplished.

the twenty-third and the twenty-seventh years too, but for ease of under-standing, I've cited the pattern of my in-laws, which is simpler. One family member of a woman dying in hospice told me that she believes that the uneven schedule was part of the "secret sauce" of its effectiveness. Because these rites do *not* occur every year, the events do not become "rote," *and* it is less likely that individual family members will skip an event, as it would be a long time before the next occasion (at least, to honor that deceased individual). "I can always go next year" becomes an impossible rationaliza-tion or deferment. So turnout is good, and the effect of binding the family together is more likely to be successful.

In both the private ritual (known as kuyō) and hōji (the public event), the basic format is the same: There is a sacred space before or within which the individual or family gathers itself and makes offerings of incense and prayer for the repose of the deceased. *Sutras*—that is, sermons by the Buddha—could be chanted (and, in the case of the larger public rites, always were). A priest officiates at the public events and might even offer a brief homily or sermon. In some Buddhist and New Religion sects, the assembled congregation also sings hymns.

Eventually, my father-in-law got wind of my pious efforts at memo-rializing my stillborn aunt and sent me a book of sutras along with the small lacquer Buddhist altar (mentioned in chapter 1), which fit nicely in a space left vacant from the removal of a window air-conditioning unit. I have a vague recollection of his attempt to teach me how to chant them when he and his wife came to dinner. Our invitation had the express pur-pose of explaining to them our plans to move back to the United States. The move was to enable me to pursue graduate study, which, happily, my father-in-law waxed enthusiastically about at the time. He phoned in the early morning hours, though, irate that we should be taking his grandson so far away! One of the saving graces of that episode was his delight in my fledgling attempts, as his daughter-in-law, to observe the ritual forms that I had so often experienced in their larger public expressions. My chanting the sutras in archaic and formal Japanese, I'm afraid, was a bit of a bridge too far (my reading out loud of any Japanese lags far behind my command of conversational Japanese, alas!), but as I have understood it, the sutra reading is actually optional.

The Chief Mourner

I don't know about you, but that already reads like a lot. And there's more! In addition to the sporadic yearly cycle of semipublic memorial events and the ongoing, private daily devotions, there are observances that form a kind of middle ground that take place closer to the death or are seasonal and span the years without interruption or syncopated scheduling, the first and most basic of which is the family priest calling on the chief mourner and whomever of the family wants to be there every week for the first seven weeks.

The chief mourner is the widow, widower, *or* the eldest son, who might be represented by his wife on occasions he cannot be present (such as the weekly rituals). He or she becomes the focal point for the ongoing ritual observances, around whom everyone else—and the family as a whole—can coalesce, and through whom each person's grieving and support can be organized and supported. I have been present at several of these weekly semiprivate rituals, but the one that stands out in my mind is the one I attended after my father-in-law's death. It was an important occasion on which one of my sisters-in-law was also in attendance, both of us hosted by the wife of the eldest son. Feelings were expressed that created both awareness and a clearing of the air. Think of how often we have that opportunity—or *not!*—and the vital exchanges that fail to transpire as a result. Or the unbounded, and therefore more perilous, offerings that can occur! The growth in depth and breadth of relationship is, in my experience, unparalleled and precious.

The Importance of Emotional Release

These weekly ritual occasions provide unmatched opportunities not only for knowing where one stands, how one is viewed, and what needs to happen to further constructive relationships within the family but are also built-in occasions for moving creatively in that direction with a minimum of extra energy or exertion, maximizing the emphasis on emotional experience. This is consistent with Confucian instruction on such matters, as in the passage from the *Analects* admonishing us to put energy into the form of the observance only to the extent that it doesn't get in the way of one's emotional catharsis.[*]

The seven weeks of weekly observances provide space and time for incremental recognition of one's feelings and those of others. One, or the family as a unit, may then be best prepared for observing the seventh of these weekly rituals (the forty-ninth day) celebrated as the official end of the first period of mourning. In biological terms, a ritual at the seventh week provides social support that gets the mourners safely past the "cumulative, time-dependent stressor effect" noticed in studies that observed greater stress at six weeks than at weeks one to three.[1] In stricter households than my own in-laws', this also marks a return to a more relaxed dietary regimen when the prescribed vegetarianism of the initial mourning period now expands to include meat. The forty-ninth-day ritual is an occasion for a more substantial, semipublic rite. This is followed by yet another semipublic ritual on the one hundredth day, then on the first anniversary, the second anniversary, and so on. In addition to these sequences, there are observances at the equinoxes. And the mid-July or mid-August observances (depending on whether you live in the Tokyo area or the Osaka/Kyoto/Kobe area of Japan), known as *Obon* (when *all* of the ancestors—not just the recently deceased—are thought to return for a few days' sojourn at the family homesteads), are the occasion for vast numbers of the Japanese traveling to their homesteads and having a much-cherished summer break.

Obon famously includes dancing at night dressed in cotton yukata and the magical, resonant, and percussive sound of wooden clogs on the

---

[*] "In ceremonies, prefer simplicity to lavishness; in funerals, prefer grief to formality" (*Analects* 3:4).

ground in a bright, festive atmosphere. In Kyoto, great fires are lit on the sides of four mountains in the shapes of characters from Buddhist philosophy (the shape of a boat to carry one to the other shore of nirvana, for instance, or the Japanese character for "big" [Dai] as in the name of the festival: Daimonji). Bundles of sticks for the fires are prepared in advance as locals write the names of deceased loved ones on them to send them via the smoke back to the other world from their brief welcome home and sojourn among the living in this world. The bundles of sticks are carried up the mountains by the eldest sons of the heads of that section of the city, reinforcing relationships and responsibilities within the civic framework. New Year's is the other seasonal time when family members visit the family graveside and express gratitude toward and concern for the collective ancestors and pray for their protection and benefaction on the living.

To complete the basic outline of the rites as the Japanese observe them, I should mention that the family events—points on the larger map—were held in a temple in the case of my in-laws, with a meal at a nearby restaurant for the assembled congregation afterward. One of my closest friends in all the world, though, held the forty-ninth-day rites with her extended family at the family homestead, with a catered meal afterward in the same room as the massive and ornate Buddhist altar, a luminescent lacquer affair all decked out in brocaded altar hangings and offerings of fruit, sweets, flowers, candles, and incense. Sure beats my little improvised setup on an empty windowsill. Such is the range of possibilities!

It seems like a lot when written out like this—and it is. But once you get the hang of it, the rituals seem not only sensible, but for some of my pilot project participants, the entire cycle felt right. The schedule of events made sense of promptings from their inner life, which urged them to observe the passing of a loved one at discrete intervals but for which no permission in the dominant culture of the United States—or form for this observation—existed. As I have described in chapter 1, one pilot participant, experiencing an impulse to this kind of observance, was even treated dismissively by people close to her. The relief she felt at being affirmed in these promptings was palpable—and may have saved her sanity!

Supporting Time to Mourn

Like nodes on a bamboo shoot, the memorial events both private and public mark time and, with any luck, growth; and more: they implicitly give permission for mourning *over* time, to *take one's time* and in that, be supported not only in one's own private ablutions but also by the social gathering of others who knew the deceased as well. Cognitive neuroscientists might call it "scaffolding"—an essential surrounding *social structure* and support for growth. It allows stories to be told, insight to surface, perspective to emerge, sensibilities to mature, and integration to occur. It provides opportunities for children to become acclimated to death and loss, to internalize the permission to feel and share those feelings; it creates a context for changes in family dynamics to unfold, become manifest, take shape, and shake out—a complete and constructive recalibration to take place.

The possibilities of the private and public rites may differ somewhat, depending on the personality of the observer and the dynamics of the family or social setting, the sect of Buddhism or other religious tradition that the family belongs to, or the region of the country in which they live. The private ritual affords more individualized gauging of the time required to be mindful and duly meditative or contemplative in the space and time that the ritual provides. Of course, it is always possible to practice mindfulness; we might say necessary, even. But in the public rites, an individual mourner cannot choose the pace at which things move, and their needs may not be met by the requirement to publicly participate. As Fenn has increasingly observed in Western culture, our need to "synchronize" with external events detracts from an awareness of ourselves and our individual needs.

Of course, this time of mourning and accompanying rites can go awry. I remember a hospice nurse in Japan telling me of the rites for her parents who had both died in hospice, leaving her alone and single at age forty.[2] The surviving family members took the occasion of the rites as an opportunity to chastise her to *chanto suru*: "do the right thing"; in her case, they were pressuring her to get married. To the best of my knowledge, it wasn't as if she were "living in sin," as the expression goes in the West—carrying on a scandalous affair right under everyone's noses or acting out in overt ways that would bring dishonor to the family. It was simply considered unsightly and improper—a disgrace, perhaps, *for* the family—for a woman to stay single. It made them nervous, maybe ashamed. Perhaps it got to the nurse because she, too, was ashamed. But it is also possible that they were thinking of her, wanted the best for her, and perceived that she needed some prodding.

With the current penchant in our culture being to chide others to "stay in your own lane," we may have lost the sensibility that informs a famous passage from the book of the prophet Isaiah, shared by both Jewish and Christian traditions. The Hebrew language provides for the recognition that such prodding *can* be a source of support and encouragement. I once heard a sermon in which the preacher noted that famous passage in Isaiah beginning, "Comfort, comfort ye, my people" and pointed out that the word "comfort" shares the same root as the word for "cattle prod!"[3]

In any event, the negative attention and the family's pressure at the public rites to conform were a disincentive for her to attend them and got in the way of her mourning her parents in that context. It interfered with her ability to be more fully present to her sadness over their deaths or other, more complex feelings that might arise because of their deaths. So she far preferred the solitary, private rite known as kuyō—the once or twice daily offerings of food and drink, prayer, and possibly the sutra chanting—where she could focus on her feelings instead of her single status and the disappointment and disapproval it generated in her relatives and the pressure that created for her.

But one bad example does not tell the full story. Nor does it do justice to the potential for these rites to be a force for good. Yet it does warn us that guidelines for their effective observance might be helpful. And now that you know more about the form the rites take, we can dive into the "content" or intent of the rites, the meditation or contemplation it supports, and the social reorganization it helps establish. In order to do that, we must start with the vital purpose of hōji and kuyō rituals—the essential release from suffering available through them.

The Misconceptions About the Rites

My friend and guide, Fukushima Keido, head abbot at the Zen teaching monastery Tofukuji in Kyoto, welcomed my interest in hōji and kuyō as a means to alleviate the suffering of Americans who have undergone a loss. But there is more to these resources than that, it turns out. He was also keen to alert me to the purpose of hōji and kuyō rituals—the ultimate release from suffering available through them.

His concern stemmed from his awareness of the distortions the Japanese themselves embraced as they undertook this ritual practice. It is a common belief—similar to our historical practices around purgatory—that survivors engage in prayer and ritual as a way of helping their deceased loved one reach "the other shore" after death—nirvana or the Pure Land. Much like my own father's insistence and many clergy and bereavement specialists in contemporary America, Keido wanted to redirect my attention to the function of the rituals for the survivors themselves. As I mentioned in the introduction, Keido taught me that the rituals were also vehicles for the survivors to become living Buddhas (not, as he colorfully intoned, for the deceased to become "dead Buddhas").

If becoming a living Buddha sounds impossibly lofty to you, you're not alone. The Japanese are very earthy, and the reality of a living Buddha is much more unpretentious than you might imagine. I find a good illustration of this point is the story Mark Epstein recounts in *Open to Desire: Embracing a Lust for Life* of psychotherapist and Buddhist teacher Jack Engler's first encounter with his guru in India. Engler had had an arduous journey but was undaunted in his eagerness for being blown away by esoteric, metaphysical propositions, or perhaps by the guru's enviable peacefulness and irreproachable aura. Instead, his guru asked Engler how his bowels were.[4]

This is a wonderful thing. But maybe not the wonderful thing that you imagine. Before describing what "becoming a living Buddha" *is*, let me clear away the underbrush of some of our own popular misconceptions—misperceptions of the role or function of meditation, for one—misunderstandings that I came across in my pilot project and beyond.

Moving Beyond the "Gates of Hell"

One common misunderstanding—a folk belief of the Japanese—involves the rationale for the schedule of ritual events. The intense, front-loaded first seven weeks of visits by the family priest are traditionally thought of as being the occasions when the survivors help the deceased get past the "six gates of hell." I have never found any official explanation for the yearly observances and their rationale; but starting with the revised idea that those six gates of hell are actually our *own* in the process of becoming living Buddhas, the yearly observances do seem to provide some cautionary protection against the wearying second year post-loss that can weigh so heavily on widows and widowers, especially.

The "seventh" year is actually observed in the sixth, as counting in matters of death is different: It begins on the day or year *before* the actual day or year, instead of proceeding *from* the actual day or year.* The seventh year for me also seems to signify the biomarkers of a complete change: It is well-known that every cell in our bodies is completely replaced in seven years, perhaps necessitating another round of recalibrating all around. Several stories in the Bible also take place in the seventh year: Jacob's reconciliation with Esau being a prime example. The thirteenth and seventeenth years stumped me for a long time, until I was led to pull out a book on insects on a shelf of books formerly owned by my grandparents and opened, serendipitously, to a page on cicadas, with their thirteen- and seventeen-year cycles. Cicadas, as you may know, are treasured pets in Japan, with little children carrying them around in plastic cages at the height of the summer.

---

* See footnote on page 72, under the section titled, "A Savvy Schedule of Grieving."

Their underground lives for such long durations and their hatching out of old carcasses suggest the process of rebirth and even resurrection; surely, most if not all of us need to shed our old ways to embrace our Buddhahood.

I haven't found a rationale for the quarter-century event (I'm open to suggestions!), but the thirty-third-year event is lauded as the last time the particular characteristics of the deceased will be felt, as they now go to join the vast assembly of generalized ancestors. From that point on, this ancestor's death anniversary will be observed at the fiftieth year and every fifty years thereafter—often along with a more recently deceased relative. The whole lends itself to a profound sense of continuity and the bonds of family—and while I'm a great fan of Henry Louis Gates's well-conceived and brilliantly executed TV program, in this system of observances, *Finding Your Roots* is hardly necessary!

The Enlightened Are Not Doormats

Keido's instruction was full of lively examples to clear away the cobwebs of our misunderstanding. There was, for instance, the story he told of being mocked by some teenage boys on the subway. Contrary to what we might assume would be the response of a monk to such mistreatment—that stereotypic imperturbability—Keido confronted the boys. "You know, if I'm a 'shitty monk,' then that makes you 'shitty kids.' Is that all right with you?" I don't remember what Keido reported as their response, but I imagine they snapped to and offered a fitting expression of remorse and apology, their heads bobbing up and down severally as they bowed and backed away in shock and embarrassment, saying, "*Sumimasen deshita!*"

If you embrace the imperturbability image of the Zen practitioner, your go-to source for commensurability in the Western canon might be the "turn the other cheek" parable of Jesus. If so, I would commend theologian Walter Wink's take on that for your consideration. Rooting his revision of our understanding of that passage in a careful study of the ethos of Jesus's day, Wink suggests that "turning the other cheek" had quite the opposite meaning from our usual sense. Instead of "bucking up in spite of mistreatment and not only taking it in stride, but going the 'extra mile,' asking, in effect, for more abuse," Wink asserts that "turning the other cheek" is decidedly *not* asking for more mistreatment, but to the contrary, refusing to be insulted by a backhanded remark and demanding to be treated with respect. Quite literally, then, "turning the other cheek" refers to the experience of being slapped by the back of someone's hand (if you can picture this: the back of the hand hitting the subject on the left cheek, an implicitly disdainful act!) and facing such an abuser straight on and pointing to the "other" (i.e., right) cheek and demanding that, if the offender has a complaint, to give it to the subject "straight"—without the disdain and, we might say, mindful of the common humanity of the subject of this abuse.[5]

Remaining Calm, Cool, and Collected Is a Myth

The image of the imperturbability of the enlightened may depend on another misconception, one espoused by the daughter of one of my pilot project participants. Susan, herself a social worker much enamored of being in touch with one's feelings, reported that her daughter appreciated meditation because it allowed one "not to feel." I can't recall anything that Keido taught explicitly on this matter, but I believe he'd share my appreciation of Francis Weller's understanding that if one doesn't allow the experience of sadness in one's life, one will not be able to experience joy, either. Meditation, rather than canceling out or elevating one above or beyond emotion, encourages a healthy respect for the full range of feeling. I'll return to this later.

You Don't Always Have to Be Polite

On the other hand, in case you expect that the well-known Zen saying "If you meet the Buddha on the road, kill him!" signals an "anything goes" permissiveness pervading the tradition, especially in terms of promptings to violence, consider Keido's instruction to his driver. Keido walked me out to the car he had waiting to take me to my next destination after one of my meetings with him. He spoke briefly to the driver. Overcome with curiosity, I asked the driver, once we got underway, what Keido had said. "Be polite" was what Keido was telling the driver as I climbed into the car. Be polite!

In my experience growing up in middle-class, White Anglo-Saxon Protestant (i.e., WASP) culture, "being polite" often translated into "nice girl" syndrome, and that, in turn, meant avoiding certain topics. Rather than finding a way to inquire politely, we have often settled, I fear, for steering clear. Jonathan Haidt's 2022 article in *The Atlantic* describes in devastating detail how that impulse—to avoid unpleasant topics or ones in which we might suffer rebuff or worse—has led to a dangerous dumbing down of our culture in general.[6] To offset the possibility of polite avoidance, I began every session of our pilot project with some "reality testing," using the reflections I'd engaged in between sessions of how something I said might have landed in ways I didn't intend or anticipate: "Last week, I said such-and-such in response to so-and-so's offering about thus and such, but I wonder if it felt like a hurtful comment to you." My aim in doing this was to remove whatever wall existed between us because of my status as an "expert" or "authority" and one that might inhibit their free expression of feeling. And my larger hope was that it modeled the ability to tolerate difficult or uncomfortable feelings even up to and including confrontation. In one of the pilot project groups, a participant expressed relief and gratitude that in that setting, no pretense was required, no avoidance of any topic or feeling state. She had attended other grief support groups and found them gimmicky, which still did not allow for a free flow of feeling and its acknowledgment. And, of course, this participant went on, normal social intercourse was far worse—almost intolerable for her at one point—in its expectation of upbeat conversation. In its more advanced and pathological forms, this type of "being polite" often spoken of recently as "toxic positivity" and entailing the avoidance of certain topics or emotions can lead to such a complete denial, suppression, or splitting off of feelings that some feelings are no longer even felt. In clinical terms, this is referred to as "dissociation."

In my life in Japan, I learned a different way. And in this, I find common ground between my Jewish and Japanese friends who were a bit more assertive and ventured forth, expressing their interest and curiosity in the healthy, honest quest of getting to know one another. Cognitive neuroscientist Dan Siegel, working at the intersection of cognitive neuroscience, attachment theory, and mindfulness, offers a counter to dissociation and a prop to better communication with a succinct acronym: COAL.[7] It stands for "curiosity, openness, acceptance, and love" as an antidote to our hamstrung conversational skills. In place of stymied subjects sidelined out of "nice girl" WASPish inhibitions, practicing curiosity, openness, acceptance, and love can offer a way through. If contemporary Christian theologian Catherine LaCugna is right and God desires the "deepest communion possible"[8] with each of us, surely that requires being open to exploring any and all topics, along with a suspension of judgment. In the sections that follow, I describe how hōji and kuyō provide a corrective context guided by constructive Confucian concepts and how the pilot project embraced and modeled this. The pilot project's participant evaluations helped me know how they received this and what it meant to them, as well as their recommendations, in turn, for you.

But there is another very important understanding of this pithy admonition to "kill the Buddha." In this era of political strongmen and self-appointed cult leaders, the Buddhist tradition warns us not to buy into their promises that they will take care of us, not to idolize them to the point of giving up our own agency. Instead, we should seek to attain our own living Buddhahood, or, as the Confucian tradition thinks of it, be sure to attend to our own "self-cultivation." Given the highly relational context of these traditions—namely, Asia and, in this case, specifically Japan—we need not read this as a hyperindividualized prompt, but merely a reminder of each person's belonging in a network of relationships. Seeking our own living Buddhahood emphasizes the need for us to take responsibility for ourselves *within* the network of relationships in which we belong with attendant duties and delights.

Assertiveness at the Expense of Others

Again, in the "what it's not" column before we go on to describe what a living Buddha is or can be, I think of the conversation I had with a colleague years ago, now, about the experience of our toddler children in their nursery school settings. I regaled her with my admiration for my son's Japanese teacher in his three-year-old nursery school class. At our group parent-teacher meeting, she told us how she went home every night contemplating how to help "little Johnny think about how his expressing himself was going to affect his friend, little Timmy."

By contrast, in her daughter's preschool setting, my colleague observed that her daughter was simply encouraged *to* express herself—without qualification or caveat, much less consideration for the other child's feelings. The other child was always referred to as "friend," a benevolent assumption that in itself held the space for the children constructively that I understand is also the case in the United States, though it wasn't part of my discussion that day with my colleague. From the age of three years old, then, Japanese children—at least, at my son's nursery school—are trained in a capacity for reflection, self-awareness, empathy, and reserve, the basic building blocks of a larger relational skill and aim: reciprocity. This practice of mindfulness at such an early age, like learning to read before starting school, surely helps get an early start on living Buddhahood—and the care needed in relationships with others. It builds a sense of the preciousness of "offering" oneself to another as opposed to simply, willy-nilly "expressing oneself" with no thought as to how one might best contribute to the relationship *through* that offering.

Not "Willfulness" or "Dominance"

One last note before I turn to describe in positive terms just what is entailed in becoming a living Buddha. For those readers who want to learn to be led by God, I direct you to Gerald G. May's best-selling book, *The Dark Night of the Soul*. May emphasizes the essential need to move away from will*fulness*—clearly attempting to affect one's ego agenda!—to willingness—a more commendable openness.[9] And besides willfulness or an unnatural calm, another attitude that a living Buddha would not exude or embrace is that of dominance. Finally, as I've mentioned earlier in the preschool example, "I'm okay and it doesn't matter if you're not" doesn't wash, either. I've grouped these together because they are different facets of the same phenomenon: our hyperindividuality. Hyperindividuality has, at its root, a failure to be sufficiently responsive and reciprocating in our relationships or mindful even in our brief, passing encounters with our fellow human beings.

Meditation Can Solve Everything

Thomas Joiner, professor of psychology at Florida State University and author of *Mindlessness: The Corruption of Mindfulness in a Culture of Narcissism*, places the failure in our current culture to be sufficiently relational at the foot of a distortion of mindfulness and the meditation practice so many embrace to achieve it. Specifically, at its having been "perverted into an excuse for self-indulgence."[10] Drawing a clear distinction between the fruits of meditation/mindfulness and the bastardized version, Joiner points out that mindfulness is *not* primarily—much less solely—about attending to one's own mind, but rather, being fully aware of "*all* of the present moment."[11] The popularity of mindfulness, Joiner asserts, is at least in part due to "there [being] both a nobility and a humility inherent in this approach to life." He writes, "It is noble in the sense that it recognizes every instance of existence, even those of great misery, as teeming and sundry. It is humble in the sense that it places the self in its proper, miniscule place within each moment's infinitude." Joiner also acknowledges mindfulness's potential to solve diverse and vexing contemporary problems, including major depressive disorder.[12] He notes that it takes *thousands* of hours of practice, so it is not a quick fix. Nor can it solve everything.

But it is worth a try. As Rollo May noted, "An extreme emphasis on individual responsibility can become an egocentric manipulation of others, a compulsion that defeats genuine morality and yields only a counterfeit sense of significance."[13] Meditation and, as I show in the next few chapters, the way it can evolve into contemplation, may be our best recourse against these dangers.

And ultimately, is it not possible, as Ernest Becker observed, "that our part of the meaning of the universe might not be a rhythm in sorrow?"[14]

So, with these myths dispensed with—what meditation cannot and should not do, who we aren't and shouldn't try to be—let's turn now to a full picture of what a living Buddha *is* and how hōji and kuyō and the meditation embedded within these rites can contribute to cultivating oneself to that end.

4

Becoming a Living Buddha

f the goal of the rituals we are discussing—hōji and kuyō—and the
meditation contained within them—is *not* about achieving personal
serenity or a culture where "anything goes," how are we to understand
the rituals' aims in positive terms? To borrow Zen Abbot Keido's concept,
which I first mentioned in the introduction, what *is* a living Buddha and
how do the Japanese rites—which are ostensibly about grieving—prepare
the practitioner and pave the way for becoming one? Allow me to remind
us that, in Keido's teaching, becoming a living Buddha is the *true* purpose
of the rites. I do not want to sell you short by neglecting to elaborate on
this important goal, even though it may seem like asking too much of the
recently bereaved. I'm hoping to show you that it isn't! Indeed, in gratitude
for Keido's teaching and supervision, I could not *fail* to touch on this most
critical point.

A Free Mind and the "Beyond"

One of Zen Abbot Keido's favorite phrases—he wrote a whole book to describe it—was "free mind."[1] What he meant was not a mind free of thought or feeling—what many budding meditators initially and erroneously believe to be the task or goal of meditating—but a mind free of *ego*. However, I think what we *actually* mean by that ambition is to eliminate "ego agenda" or "attachment to the ego." Because we all need an ego to get things done: what is often referred to as "ego strength." As we've seen, the "beyond" that hōji, kuyō, and meditation generally strive to reach is not the beyond usually referred to as "the afterlife" or a realm we enter following physical death. And, again, it does not refer to being devoid of all thinking and emotion. Rather, the beyond we aim for is the realm of experience governed by getting past the *grasping* and *domineering tendencies* of the ego—the vain effort (in both senses of the word) to establish a fixed (as opposed to fluid) "identity." An identity that appeals to our ego but may not be in line with the truth about ourselves and the way things are in general—the basic unity and interrelatedness of all things.

But what does *this* "beyond" look like in positive terms? And what does one *do* in and from this beyond? According to Keido, therein lies simply the ability *to respond spontaneously to any and all situations appropriately*. Many positive psychologists speak of "flow"—a state achieved when a person forgets oneself and is caught up in a task at once pleasant and challenging. That flow is very close to what Keido has in mind here, although Keido's application is more general, applying not only to one task, but to *all* things as a person goes about their ordinary day.

In this fluid state—the state characterizing a living Buddha—it should be noticed, mindfulness is not *mindlessness*. It is not absent *mind*—that is, all the functions of the mind—much less is it absent "care." Nor is it—or one's identity—devoid of continuity. What is absent is *calculation*. Famously, it is acting without attachment to the outcome of the action or even—perhaps most particularly—attachment to the *image* created *of us* by so acting. In short, minus an ego agenda.

Imagine what it would be like to always be spontaneously appropriate. A friend of mine recently regaled me with his joy at having finally learned not to act out—to yell, cast blame, and criticize unhelpfully. Together we observed that this was a two-fer: Not only did it spare him the agony, time, and effort of the repair needed when he did behave in this way, but it allowed for positive activities to flourish instead. This is a small example of what Keido was referring to: the ability to be appropriate spontaneously. No need to defend one's ego or promote the image it would prefer to be its proxy. Undercutting those very common but unhelpful aims, my friend was unusually sensitive and wanting to do right, especially in his relationship with his wife, where his acting out occurred. But there are times when we err inadvertently—of which we mostly remain unaware, even though the damage is done. Perhaps you can recall examples from your own experience where you sensed something wasn't quite right but didn't know how to go about addressing it. Imagine being free of these habits—not of the heart, but of the ego and its desire to dominate, be right, control with its resultant doubts, anxieties, alienations, and depression. If there are microaggressions, there are accompanying microinjuries that afflict the afflicter as well as the afflicted. Imagine being free of such trouble: of one's mind being released from these agonies. A free mind.

The Ego Agenda Versus Our Emotions

It might help to explore some examples of an ego agenda and how it arises in the context of these ritual observances. We might also ask how these ritual observances help offset the dangers of an ego agenda. My in-laws' priest, Yamasaki Akio, whom I consulted as I began my dissertation research, warned of a kind of "keeping up with the Joneses" mentality that can creep into hōji observances. The priest spoke of witnessing the puffed-up pride produced by outdoing one's acquaintances in lavish displays and elaborate memorial occasions.

Another example of an ego agenda and what might lie beyond refers to Buddhism's eightfold path, which includes refusing to put others down in an attempt to puff oneself up. My in-laws' priest, Yamasaki-sensei, illustrated this with a story about a couple of his parishioners who complained to him during his visit on a memorial occasion at their house. Having seen an article in the newspaper about their sister-in-law's work, they were filled with a venomous desire to denigrate her work to continue in their pompous but empty pride. Yamasaki described this by using compelling contrasts: "They are materially rich, but spiritually poor." I appreciated his delicate discernment and recognition of the difference between material poverty and spiritual poverty. He offered this as an example in answer to my curiosity about the kind of questions or issues his parishioners present during his visits to conduct the memorial occasions held in the home during the first seven weeks of bereavement. In light of Keido's concern about ego agendas, it is clear that these sisters were hamstrung by clinging to their faltering egos in light of someone else's achievement, sadly unable to partake of the joy in it and contribute to it but determined to detract from it exactly as prohibited in Buddhist doctrine.

It's clear that an ego agenda can drive a mourner's actions, rather than that person using the opportunity of the ritual to experience their emotions. A grieving person's exploration of emotions allows the person to release their feelings by either expressing them or simply being aware of them. If the person allows understanding and self-discovery to emerge, their journey can result in a positive recalibration of relationships as the constellation of those relationships changes after the departure of the deceased. As the Confucian classic the *Analects* points out, simple emotion is far preferable to elaborate display—display being a function of the ego and an attempt to create an image of oneself rather than humbly *being* oneself. Keido warned of the opposite tendency as well: a stinginess that withholds an appropriate tribute for the sake of saving money in a miserly manner—to spend on oneself in some imagined future.

There are shades and *shades* of potential for displays of ego agenda: wanting to be *seen* as being appropriate rather than spontaneously *doing* the appropriate. *In what ways might you be tempted*, I wonder, *to allow your ego to dominate and determine your actions?*

Emotion and Form

In the rituals, the method and actual objects offered are less important than the offerer's mind and heart—how or why they made the offering. Confucius's admonishment to place more importance on emotion than form was in the back of my mind one particular day when I was serving on the faculty and administration of an Episcopal seminary. I was responsible for modeling a priest's role in conducting our main ritual, known as the Eucharist, or the celebration of the Last Supper. While conducting the Eucharist that morning, it seemed to be my fate to make every mistake possible throughout the ritual. But with each blunder, I improvised, and most importantly, showed my seminary students that making those sorts of slips was not the end of the world. One student liturgist, responsible for planning and then critiquing the Eucharist, noted everything I had done wrong and my improvisations, which he then enthusiastically pronounced had "worked!"

The Confucian emphasis on emotion over form is, I believe, well matched by the Anglican insistence on the importance of "intention." If I had to articulate my intention as a priest conducting liturgy, it is decidedly *not* to be flawless in execution (though perfection would be nice!), but to be an instrument or vehicle of grace.

Putting more emphasis on emotion than form may help us move toward a positive definition or description of a living Buddha, or a life modeled on Christ as one example of a rough equivalence. Participating in memorial events for their cathartic potential rather than something more egocentric—such as putting on a show and forgetting about one's grief—also moves one toward that desired goal.

Yet when emotions are too complex or difficult, and a person hasn't had adequate support or scaffolding to recognize and accept those emotions, that person might employ all manner of defense against them—denial, deflection, dissociation. As you may recall, Freud warned against ambivalence as an impediment to working through grief, possibly leading to a lingering, debilitating condition he called melancholy.[2]

These strategies to ignore our feelings get in the way of our being able to be "spontaneously appropriate," as we can't consciously choose how to deal with and handle those emotions. In addition, the act of denying our emotions can exert an undue influence, distorting our perception and our responses to reality. In a seminar I conducted at Westminster Abbey following the death of Princess Diana, it was crystal clear that much of the participants' feelings with respect to the princess were a cumulative effect of many other bereavements that they hadn't had appropriate support to cope with and grow from.

The ideal of the living Buddha helps with grief by providing a lofty yet attainable end goal. Without it, Sunny, Ruth, Mariah, Dave, Katie, and countless others were—and may still be—casting about for guidance. It is too difficult, after all, to get beyond the ego unless one knows—or at least has a plausible idea of—what lies beyond—again, in positive terms. In counseling, a therapist is careful not to dismantle a client's defenses until something better is put in place.

As psychologist William James famously observed, we are all naturally "conservative"—that is, we prefer *not* to change, unless not changing is more painful than changing.[3] Death and loss of any kind put us in an unavoidable situation of change, so being prodded to an admirable end is, in my experience, comforting. I am often surprised—but delighted—when bereaved folks I work with agree to, and are actually thrilled at, the prospect of my sharing their story with others. On the one hand, I might expect their egos to be self-protective and refuse to give me permission. But almost universally, there is a sense of gratification at the implicit participation in "spiritual recycling." Despite whatever embarrassment might be inherent in the experience, the thought of helping another person overcomes any shame.

So how do we move beyond an ego agenda and instead let our emotions take up their appropriate space, time, and intensity when we grieve?

From Meditation to Contemplation

And what about a more general approach? What other hints are there for what lies beyond an ego agenda, and how do we get there? Psychiatrist and theologian Gerald G. May, whose observation of the move from "willfulness" to "willingness" that I mentioned in the previous chapter, makes that distinction in his larger argument for meditation yielding to a wider, more open and welcoming process he calls "contemplation." Indeed, one makes the move *from* meditation to contemplation by "welcoming with open arms" the experiences of God, which one *cannot* bring about by an effort of will. In other words, we come to recognize that this welcoming is a kind of receptivity, not activity, and decidedly *not* a function of egoic effort, but rather often in spite of or beyond it.[4]

Meditation, in a sense, is preparing the ground for this broader openness. And meditation most often entails experiencing the notions that the ego has kept at bay: difficult emotions and feelings, thoughts, and impulses not commensurate with the image one has or would like to project about oneself. Indeed, it's helpful to realize that meditation is having its desired effect *not* when one feels *nothing* or only pleasant emotions, but precisely when one feels *bad*, unpleasant, or undesirable feelings! Meditation is a process of making room for *all* of oneself, without judgment.

On a more basic level, many of my friends who have tried a bit of meditation are flummoxed at the notion that they have to halt the mind from doing what it does, to *stop thinking*. Instruction in meditation, I'm happy to see, has improved since I conducted my pilot project, and the task of "emptying the mind" is less and less about forcing the mind not to think or feel, but about allowing the space, time, and discipline to actually see the mind in action—namely, to observe its grasping tendencies, its desires to present oneself in a certain light, to be right, superior, or good.

Gerald G. May tells how thirteenth-century mystics Teresa of Ávila and John of the Cross went through a process of "learning to be led." In his own experience, he learned that one's labeling of experience as "bad" or "good" can be temporary and deeply misleading, since so-called "bad" experiences can ultimately yield the greatest lessons and deepest happiness, and vice versa.

Francisco Varela, an early pioneer working at the intersection of meditation, cognitive neuroscience, and Buddhism, describes an important stage of becoming adept at meditation. At a certain point, Varela says, the meditator relaxes "further into awareness" where "a sense of warmth and inclusiveness dawns." He writes:

> The street fighter mentality of watchful self-interest can be let go somewhat to be replaced by interest in others. We are already other-directed even at our most negative, and we already feel warmth toward some people, such as family and friends. The conscious realization of the sense of relatedness and the development of a more impartial sense of warmth are encouraged in the mindfulness/awareness tradition by various contemplative practices such as the generation of loving-kindness. It is said that the full realization of groundlessness (sunyata) cannot occur if there is no warmth.[5]

The warmth Varela points to represents a distinct stage in the meditator's process. I mention it here as a signpost along the way—for both the observer and the practitioner—to know they are on the right path. It distinguishes the meditator with only a cerebral or intellectual grasp of the practice from someone who's made notable progress and may be on to something worthwhile. The appearance of warmth occurs when one passes the point of the oft-touted "emptiness," which is a kind of nihilism. So strong is our need to grasp and try to hold on to *something* that we will desperately do so, even if that *something* is actually *nothing*!

A light went on when I read this: I had experienced my father as nihilistic. He was so afraid of his ego and pride that he was determined his children wouldn't suffer a similar struggle. As a result, he undercut everything we did—never praising and always finding fault, in a vain and misguided hope to protect us from his own fate. The definitive experience was when I brought home a report card with all A's and one A-minus. My father's only comment to me was, "What's the minus?" Admittedly, this example might be considered mild, but cumulatively, it took a toll.

My oldest sister began to embody this trait early on: When I was five years old and expressed my dream of becoming a ballerina, she told me I would get fat thighs. I don't think I even knew what a thigh was at that age, but the tone was unmistakable: Whatever happened to the thighs was bad and must be avoided at all costs. Similarly, my father squelched my dream as a ten-year-old of becoming a violinist: "It's a lonely life," he said. So perhaps you can see how that instruction gave us nowhere to stand, nothing to value, nothing to become invested in, even—and especially—our own lives. In trying to prevent us from becoming prideful or too attached to our egos, our father effectively stunted our growth of *any* ego in the sense of *ego strength*. But one cannot get *beyond* an ego that isn't fully developed. The need for an ego to be well-developed *before* it could be overcome in spiritual disciplines was a relatively well-known trope in the '70s.

I am grateful for Varela's appreciation of warmth for another reason. It explains my distaste when I overheard a conversation between a fellow patient in my acupuncturist's office and the receptionist about recent political developments. The patient, with feigned concern for the world, stated coldly that she would be okay "because I meditate," though she also clearly meant that others who didn't practice meditation would *not* be okay. I guess she hadn't reached the level of "inclusiveness" to which Varela points, which presumes, "If they're not okay, I'm not okay." Varela goes on to describe other traditions, the Mahayana, for instance, where spiritual growth is approached from the opposite direction. Rather than beginning with meditation, growth begins with the conscious cultivation of compassion.

I hadn't placed much emphasis on meditation in my pilot project, and in hindsight, I became quite anxious that I may have blown it. I had set out with a largely unconscious understanding that my work was to take what the participants offered as the fruit of their rituals and contemplations at their altars or at the altar of their minds (to quote Marianne Williamson) and probe it for the compassion it would eventually yield.

Susan's surprising empathy for her long-lost cousins, Rickie's resignation of the blame she attributed to her brother, Charles's relinquishing his claim on an old flame—these are all acts of self-emptying—*kenosis*, in Christian theological terms—of the sort Keido would commend, I reckoned: compassion and a recognition, a reverence, if you will, for the life of another and the integrity of their own choices. And, ultimately, a free mind, available for whatever is to come without debilitating obsessions, addictions, or misplaced convictions. Hard-won, to be sure. Requiring an investment of time and effort, indeed. And not attained without the support of interested—nonjudgmental, open, curious, accepting—others. I had experienced this in Japan and wanted to bring it home and share.

For some time in my own process, I clung to the pithy summary in which Varela synthesizes the emptiness approach with the cultivating of compassion in this catchy phrase: "Emptiness is full of compassion."[6]

Where that is *not* the case, conversely, one can safely assume that the ego is at work. And that more work—on getting beyond it—is needed! While compassion is needed to become a living Buddha, it is my experience that it is also necessary to grieve effectively, completely, and fully. I believe it is safe to say that where compassion is lacking, for *anyone* else, it is lacking for ourselves. And this must not be allowed to stand! We deserve compassion, even if we cannot earn it. And a succinct passage from the *Analects* again serves as a barometer and a compass: how we're doing, where to look, and on what to focus. Put me in a room with any two people and invariably I'll have something to learn: from the good, I'll take a model, from the bad, I'll take a warning.[7]* This can be read as a warning to look to ourselves for the qualities we may be reviling in the other and to find it within ourselves to go beyond

---

* When I started pursuing this as a spiritual discipline, I would ask when I myself might have behaved in the offensive way that I am reviling in another. That would form the basis for me both to be humble instead of blaming or hating and have compassion for and curiosity about the other.

our contempt, hatred, or disdain and eventually arrive at compassion—first, for oneself, from which it can radiate outward to all. While difficult and not frequently attained, this, I suggest, is what Keido was instructing as the end of all grief—the appropriate aim and goal toward which all the rituals and resources combine to effect. Beyond our ambivalences. Beyond the mechanics of ritual. Beyond ourselves.

I like that word "beyond." It doesn't suggest or advocate annihilation, denial, suppression, oppression, repression, or castigation. Just moving through, perhaps, and past. Like Aikido for the ego! It suggests that ego is, in fact, foundational, but not sufficient in itself and must, rather, be like a stepping stone to some greater realm of awareness and experience. Not *after this life*, but squarely situated within it. Part of its flow. Or, we might say, participating *in* its flow.

How else might we understand and aspire to become a living Buddha? While helpful and instructive, we need not stop at Keido's example of the qualities of a living Buddha. Or Varela's warnings about meditation that fails its purpose and the signposts of its hitting the mark.

Learning to Be Led

While warmth is an important indicator that we are on our way to achieving the results that meditation promises, we mustn't stop there. Our ultimate goal is ridding ourselves—not of our ego, per se, but of its dominance, as it can get in the way of more ultimate goods: the fruit of the Spirit or being in flow and responding appropriately in any and all circumstances. In place of ego dominance, many throughout the ages have understood this as the process of learning to be led: only in this practice do we approach participating in the flow that Keido commends and sets out as our true end. We have met May in his commending *willingness* in place of *willfulness* as a marker of the difference between using meditation to proper ends—or not. He also means it as a discernment in the general project of overcoming the dominance of the ego. His recommendation is part of his project in writing about the thirteenth-century mystics John of the Cross and

Teresa of Ávila, whom he takes as his models in learning how to be led. The ultimate goal for mystics is ecstatic union with God. We may see this as the proper culmination of that Confucian prescription or progression from knowing, through loving, and finally to delight. To know something is not as good as to love it; to love something is not as good as to delight in it.[8] May describes a critical moment for these mystics, when *meditation* gave way to *contemplation*: the simple act of being open to God's presence. May's understanding corresponds nicely with Keido's concept of "free mind." May describes it this way:

> Whatever form it takes, the movement of the soul and God is always finding its way toward freedom. In prayer as in the rest of life, it is a movement toward freedom from willfulness, from the compulsion to be in charge and the fear of loss of control. It is a movement toward freedom from "functional atheism," the conviction that effortful autonomous accomplishment is the only hope. And it is a movement toward freedom *for* the simple loving presence and appreciation, a willingness to respond and participate in the divine Spirit in the world, a trusting confidence that allows radically loving action.[9]

Later, he cites the Buddhist concept of compassion in a way that describes how spontaneous and appropriate action is possible in the way Keido describes: "Some Buddhists say that true compassion is the essence of creation. Thus, if allowed to remain free from our own ego agendas, it will arise directly and spontaneously within every situation."[10]

Taken together, May's understanding of "a willingness to respond and participate in the divine Spirit in the world, a trusting confidence" and the explicitly noted freedom "from our own ego agendas" is more than a rough equivalent of Keido's cry to respond with compassion—even "radically loving," as Keido demonstrated in his approach to the teenage boys who harassed him.

I love May's understanding of some Buddhist traditions' notion "that true compassion is the essence of creation." For our purposes—doing better at bereavement and especially in its social aspects—I find compassion, as in suffering with, particularly helpful. "Love"—with its wildly differing definitions and usages ("I just *love* that dress!")—benefits by being seen through the lens of this rough equivalence. "Suffering with" draws attention to our common experience, our relatedness, our mutuality, and our reciprocity. It liberates us from any pretensions we might have to fix or prescribe, to identify the stage one is in, even to hug rape someone who is bereaved. It allows us to set aside the ego agenda for the simple experience of being with, in the abundant hope that, in so doing, the compassion that is the essence of creation will arise directly and spontaneously.

A Confucian would not bother to speculate on the essence of creation, but Keido and May's insistence on getting beyond one's ego agenda seems to presuppose such a metaphysics.

Gerald G. May isn't the only Christian—or psychiatrist—to testify to a mysterious metaphysical underpinning that makes possible our trust and reliance on it, even abandoning our limiting ego agenda for the chance to be a vehicle of something greater that allows love, peace, and joy. Mark Epstein, in his highly original thesis on the nature of the Buddha's enlightenment, cites Michael Eigan, a psychiatrist, who writes, "If you penetrate to the core of your aloneness you will not only find yourself, there will also be this unknown boundless presence. Is it you? Is it other than you? What is it? An unknown, boundless presence at the very core of your aloneness."[11]

I have had my own unique ego experience. To treat my postpartum depression, I began therapy with a Japanese woman psychiatrist—one of only three in the whole country at the time who worked on a Western fifty-minute talk therapy model. I expressed my envy of my eldest sister, imagining that her husband and two children spared her the loneliness I was feeling. My psychiatrist, Dr. Kobayashi, asked, "Don't you think she has her own loneliness?" And with that, I felt myself mentally descend into a deep well, falling, falling through the darkness until a bright, effulgent light burst forth from what would have been the bottom—from the direction *of* the bottom—which I never hit because I became enveloped in this powerful, embracing light.

Dr. Kobayashi reminded me of my sister's humanity, our common bond in it, all while enabling me to face my fear, my sense of being alone— utterly alone. Once I had fully faced it, the pain dispersed in the light, which became for me a beacon of hope—a kind of metaphysical experience that I have never forgotten. A conversion event, in essence.

Perhaps because of that striking event, I believed that spiritual gifts— since they are given and not "achieved"—occurred naturally, without effort on our part. I got my comeuppance on this in a conversation with Keido in which he set me straight. No, he instructed; it takes intention. In fact, a sign hanging over the great meditation hall that stood in the center of his temple compound reads, "Choose the Buddha." When my brother-in-law and I were taken on a tour of the grounds by one of Keido's apprentice monks, my brother-in-law was unabashedly taken aback by this. "It's a *choice*?" he asked the novice. I was taken aback in turn by his sincerity in posing the question, by his willingness to reveal his not having known this. A commanding presence, he had never been this open, this perplexed, this receptive in front of me.* And I loved him in that moment as I had never loved him before. This episode was also a perfect illustration of the way that the Confucian tradition originating in China was "trojanized" into Japanese Buddhism (and the Rinzai sect in particular) through monks' assiduous study of Confucian texts over centuries. A Confucian would recognize this movement of my own heart and mind and a new appreciation for my brother-in-law; arrogance wins hatred, after all, while modesty wins love.

Many of the prompts I gave the pilot project participants were passages from Confucian classics, usually the *Analects*. The *Analects* and other

---

* The late British theologian John Hull identified the difficulty Christians have in learning as lying in the unwillingness to admit that they don't know, which is preliminary to having the requisite openness that May commends. See Hull's *What Prevents Christian Adults from Learning?* (Hymns Ancient & Modern Ltd, 2012).

Confucian classics were memorized by Japanese schoolchildren until after World War II. Japan then tried to purge the country of Confucian influence, blaming it for the weakness in their culture that led to their defeat. As with most religious or spiritual traditions, historical factors can lead to emphases *within* the tradition that skew how it gets promulgated and can have unintended or unhealthy consequences. Some of the conservatism blamed on the Confucian tradition, I would suggest, is a function of interpretation and ego-driven agenda at the helm of that interpretation. Such historical tangents and forces, in my humble opinion, should not become the basis for a wholesale dismissal of it, which contains many salvageable and salvific riches.

In terms of May's description and prescription of how to go about learning to be led—to participate in that radical love—he also warns that time, practice, and above all, *intention*, are required. For May, receptivity is key. It is the marker of the transition from meditation to contemplation. Since it is the move from will*ful*ness to will*ing*ness, the most one can do is *welcome* it, be open to it, and *be receptive* to it. An accomplished person, my brother-in-law is used to calling the shots, telling people what to do, being the boss, and actively pursuing his goals. He may have vaguely been aware that the realm of spirituality *does* involve receptivity, and in my experience, Japanese culture as a whole is far more willing to embrace a receptive mode. So within that, it may have seemed strange that a choice was required. But mastery of the ego is always a choice, a discipline, a willingness. In that way, it involves us and our power *to* choose, even though we ironically are powerless to bring about the actual event. Hōji and kuyō, then, are vehicles, occasions, and opportunities *for* that receptivity to bear fruit. They require, and provide the scaffolding for, as both May and Keido would assert: time, practice or repetition, and, above all, intention.

But May is clear that we, as human beings, can *never* know the full meaning or significance of an event, however good and clear our intention. A well-known Zen parable perfectly illustrates this concept: A farmer experiences bad luck, about which his neighbors come to commiserate with him. "So tragic!" they say, to which he says, "Maaaaaybe," and the supposedly "bad" event turns out to have a silver lining, bringing about some great good fortune that would otherwise not have occurred. The neighbors come around this time to congratulate him. "Isn't it wonderful," they intone. And again, his response is, "Maaaaaybe . . . ," and this cycle repeats ad infinitum. May offers some markers to assist us in our efforts to learn to be led and to detect if we're on the right track, but, he carefully asserts, we can never assume that what we *believe* is our being led is, in fact, that.*

Uncertainty and the Necessity of Humility

And since we can never be sure we are on the right track, even as we may trust and feel that we are, I am convinced that Rickie was right in encouraging me to include the polite form I mentioned before as a way of hedging our bets, building those bridges, and further cultivating in us a steering away from our ego agenda's hold on us. *Sumimasen deshita* is a Japanese phrase for an acknowledgment of those cracks where the light gets in. Or, as in the Japanese aesthetic *kintsugi*, a strengthening where we would normally see weakness and be afraid.

But politeness as a requisite in positive social interactions is part of a larger theme, a more basic awareness and key variable to success in a social realm or even in the effort to allow oneself to be led: humility. Concerning habits of humility, I'm willing to venture that the Japanese (while they may not always live up to it or practice it faithfully) have mastered the art with various disciplines that they introduce from a child's earliest days. And hōji and kuyō are part of these practices.

British theologian John Hull has written a compelling treatise on the importance of humility in his *What Prevents Christian Adults from Learning?*[12] If the purpose of grieving is to grow and the rites we are discussing

* I've listed May's markers to our discipline in learning to be led in Appendix C.

are to support that, then an openness to learning would seem requisite. Richard Rohr, founder of the Center for Action and Contemplation, prolific writer, and Franciscan priest, pointed out that the need to be right is the critical impediment to learning.[13] So habits of humility—acknowledging our faults, being open to the possibility of it to begin with—can be seen as crucial in creating the kind of openness that encourages honest sharing of emotion and perspective. Habits of humility also create the openness necessary for receptivity on all levels, not just between fellow survivors or humanity in general, but in our intuitions and as we perceive our environment.

Part of the humility entailed in learning to be led is the recognition that achieving that participation in flow is not a one-and-done endeavor. To the contrary! Even for an accomplished mystic such as Teresa of Ávila, Gerald G. May reports that such a state lasts a maximum of thirty minutes at any given time. Keido gave me one of his calligraphic scrolls of a pithy Zen statement: A garden needs constant weeding; the weeds of an ego agenda always grow back and require constant vigilance.

Well-known spiritual teacher Wayne Dyer illustrated this concept with self-deprecating humor: He found a list that informed him that he was the third most popular spiritual guru of our time, a finding he came across on the internet. Dyer explained that the ego started to ask, "Who are these people who are more spiritually influential than you, and how are you going to take them down?" With the Dalai Lama at number one and Eckhart Tolle at number two, Dyer joked, "I figure Eckhart and I maybe can get together and take the Dalai Lama out of this thing."[14]

Keido had told me that even after enlightenment, one must "return to the dualistic world"—the world of good and evil and the constant demand to discern, decide, and act. In *An Interpretation of Christian Ethics*, Reinhold Niebuhr posits that the real meaning of the story of Adam and Eve is *not* that nakedness is wrong or the human body sinful or even that Eve is a temptress, but rather the cost of conscience.[15] Being banished from the garden illustrates the pain of our human struggle with our conscience—our awareness that there *is* a difference between good and evil, even if it isn't always clear where the line is. Humankind's subsequent learning to be led would entail a long and bloody history, culminating in the so-called "Second Adam," as Christ is often called, who came to show us how to be receptive to the promptings of the spirit in union with all things, which prevents us from acting on our evil impulses.

If receptivity allows meditation to become contemplative and compassion to arise, receptivity also provides a context for the cultivation of reverence. But now that we've discussed becoming a living Buddha and its relation to conscience and the grieving process, it's finally time to turn to a deeper engagement with an intriguing analysis of the life and discipline of the historical Buddha—one that, you'll be interested to know, involves an early and painful loss—that of his mother.

5

How the Historical Buddha
Grieved (or Didn't)

n the previous chapter, we began to explore the Zen Head Abbot Keido's instruction as to the ultimate purpose of the rituals we have been
looking at: to become a living Buddha—the ultimate goal of life itself.
Becoming a living Buddha allows us to respond to every situation spontaneously and appropriately and in this way eliminate unnecessary suffering
brought about by our mindless acts, our carelessness, our being out of
touch with reality, and what others or ourselves might truly need. It is the
manifestation of our oneness with all things and the source of the deepest
bliss. But let us now turn to the role of a "holding environment," or the pro-
ductive part that others can play in supporting an individual toward this
lofty end, inspiring the cultivation of character and the spiritual aspiration
to Buddhahood or, for example, a life modeled on Christ.*

---

* The phrase, "holding environment," was coined by British psychiatrist D. W. Winnicott,
  perhaps the foremost successor to and elaborator on the insights of Ian Suttie, though
  many who know Winnicott's work are unaware of Suttie's influence on him.

Mark Epstein's insightful guide to the Buddha's own enlightenment is rooted in the early loss of the Buddha's mother. Epstein's account elucidates the profound effect of social support—or its lack—from within the Buddhist tradition itself. The Buddha's path to enlightenment, while attempting to follow the instructions of the gurus of his day, essentially relied on his own efforts. And many of us who are grieving believe, even when supported by family and friends, that "getting over" or "recovering" or "moving on" is basically up to us and a robust effort. Models of grief outlined in chapter 2 describe that effort, but not the kind of support that might be helpful. We might be—and I often am—tempted to see this as a function of the hyperindividualism of our day, but intriguingly, that individual effort is present even in the time—and mind—of the historical Buddha. So our own enlightenment—as well as progress with grieving—is best aided not only by social support, but by a certain *type* of support, as well as our particular attitude and set of behaviors. Yet often, things get in our way of embracing the appropriate attitudes and embodying the helpful behaviors that the Buddha's own experience illustrates and commends.

The Buddha's road to enlightenment began when he left his home and his sheltered life as a prince—abandoning his wife and child at the palace for a lengthy apprenticeship in everything on offer in the spiritual landscape of his day. He went from asceticism to hedonism and back again, trying to find peace—a way to rise above the suffering inherent in existence. Having lived an exceptionally sheltered life as a prince, his only conscious experience of hardship at that point was abstract and external: in his coming across living examples of aging, illness, and death on a rare trip outside the palace.

Epstein's analysis suggests that the Buddha left home in large part because of the failure of his family to provide a holding and healing environment following the loss of his mother, when he was only six days old. This lack of support drove his grief underground and doomed him for a time in the cycle of repeating, compulsively, the original abandonment. The possibility of this harmful cycle was why it was so important for

Sunny to provide constructive support to her friend and for Mariah to "get it right" with her own grieving! Making the world safe for sorrow entails creating contexts where we don't need to suppress our thoughts and feelings, giving them the power to exert an uncontrolled and uncontrollable destructive influence.

Memories, Dreams, and Enlightenment

During the historical Buddha's spiritual quest, at a point when he was particularly emaciated, six years into his attempt to follow the disciplines of his day, a spontaneous memory occurred to him, followed by a series of five dreams. The memory was of a moment of particular bliss, when he was a child in a rose-apple tree. The Buddha realized that this feeling of bliss was not a result of striving or accomplishment or anything external—gifts, glamour, birth, education, status, or the like. The feeling instead seemed to him foundational—that is, the essence of life inherent in the process of living, a metaphysical reality—available to all and able to arise spontaneously, if only we would allow it and recognize it as such. The memory included the awareness of the interrelatedness of all things and their inherent beauty and splendor.

The Buddha's dreams signified to him that, contrary to his previous attempts to *deny* his physicality and connection with all that is on this plane of existence in the hopes of reaching and sustaining bliss through his own efforts, he was decidedly—inherently—related to everything. And the Buddha realized that denying this was doing him more harm than good. His attempt to escape parts of his experience was the source of his pain and suffering—a delusion he had to overcome. Not by attempting to transcend the demands of the flesh through esoteric practices, but by attending to both his physicality and his relationality, simply and mindfully.

The actual nature of life is bliss, the Buddha saw, but this bliss is too often obscured by our habitual misperceptions. The egocentric life is suffering, the Buddha realized. This life is conditioned by conceit and needs a self to be built up and protected and separated out, in its own version of dissociation, from the rest of the universe.* The Buddha's discovery was not of suffering, but of freedom and of relatedness.[1]

The bliss of which the Buddha spoke was, needless to say, not only *not* the bliss of dissociation, such as that reached through yoga or meditation, but even less that of drugs, addiction, distraction, or denial (and certainly not President Bush's acquiescence to the "consumerist heart" in his admonition to go "shopping" in the aftermath of 9/11).

Epstein sums it up this way, using the Buddha's historical name, also spelled Gautama:

> [Gautama's] experiences [of the transcendental practices of yoga and meditation on the one hand and self-punishment on the other, two strains of spiritual striving (that) have a long history in South Asia] reinforced his tendency toward dissociation by removing him even more completely from his body and everyday mind, but they removed him in a way that left his preoccupation with the traumatic underpinnings of life untouched.[2]

At this critical juncture, just after his spontaneous memory and the five dreams, the Buddha had a chance encounter with a woman who had come to the spot where he was meditating. She offered him a bowl of gruel, and, realizing he was going to need sustenance to complete his path to enlightenment, the Buddha partook of the meal with gratitude. Yet the five friends who had stood by him and cheered him on during his six-year pursuit of extreme ascetic discipline were disgusted by his capitulation to the "things of this world" and abandoned him as he ate the gruel.

---

* This separation—from self, other, world and, for Christians, God—is what Christians understand by the word "sin." Sin is *not* in the first instance bad acts, but rather, the state of separation that gives rise to such acts. Overcoming this separation is our most basic longing. And what Epstein's analysis helps us understand how to achieve.

The Cost of the Lack of a Holding Environment

Epstein doesn't make much of the abandonment of Buddha's so-called friends—but this is of interest to us, given Sunny's initial and urgent request to be guided on how to be a *good* friend to Mariah in her grief and our focus on the social aspect of grieving.

Much of the literature on bereavement in the United States discusses the sometimes downright awful things that people say—or do—to those who are recently bereaved, often in a misguided attempt to offer comfort and consolation, if only to themselves. Recall Mariah's discomfort with the assumption by some that she wanted—*needed*—a hug, which she came to call hug rape. Well-meaning but misguided attempts to console in their basic bumbling are what I will label here as "irreverence."

Still, a holding environment is requisite. Epstein sums it up this way: "Trauma becomes sufferable, even illuminating, when there is a relational home to hold it in. Without this, it is simply too much to bear."[3]

We have had a glimpse of this phenomenon, this truth, in Lindemann's earliest studies of battlefield healing: soldiers who were injured did much better when allowed to recuperate *on the battlefield*, in the company of those who clearly understood what the injured were going through and could implicitly hold it with them.

Epstein notes that it's not just *any* social context, but one within which a person's feelings can be verbalized, understood, and held by those around them. Without such a holding environment, the costs are dire. Epstein writes, "The shock of trauma sits outside awareness like a coiled spring."[4] If that isn't enough to inspire trepidation and make you wonder if the world is safe from your sorrow, and you from the sorrow of others, he goes on:

> The emotions aroused—which by their very "unbearable" nature cannot be imagined—are left unexplored. The self that moves forward is restricted by its failure to integrate the traumatic impact, by its failure to process its unbearable feelings. In its attempts to "ensure that what has already happened is

unlikely ever to be repeated in the same way," the defense of dissociation splits the self into a fiefdom of incompatible states.[5]

It's worth noting here that Epstein's focus and concern is on the input that becomes unavailable from other "parts of the self" when dissociation takes hold; but it can and equally should be said that a dissociated self also resists input from other people. Unless certain conditions prevail, that is. We will pursue this a bit further in a moment. In the meantime, begin to imagine that *this* is another—if not *the*—source of our currently fragmented and deeply defensive collective society.

Rollo May presciently prophesied our current preoccupation with violence as a function of dissociation and a longing for ecstasy that corresponds uncannily with the Buddha's experience:

> Now when we consider contemporary man—insignificant, lonely, more isolated as mass communication becomes vaster . . . aware of his identity only to the extent that he has lost it, yearning for community but feeling awkward and helpless as he finds it—when we consider this modern man, who will be surprised that he yearns for ecstasy even of the kind that violence and war may bring?[6]

Richard Rohr further adds this empathic note: "Evil is really goodness tortured by its own hunger and thirst, goodness that has not been able to experience being received and given back . . . . 'Evil' is what happens when human beings become tortured with this desire for goodness that they cannot experience."[7]

The Healing Sense of Presence

In Epstein's further elucidation of the Buddha's experience, he shows that the Buddha found within his dreams a maternal presence, a nurturing that ultimately enabled him to return to who he was before the rupture of his trauma. And he was finally able to see that his mother's death was *not* a result of his having been bad—the quintessential thought/feeling of a child who goes through a loss—but rather a result of her tremendous love, operating at a frequency so highly charged that her frail physique failed her. She could only contain the love she felt by becoming an astral body and leaving this plane of existence.

Having recovered not only a sense of his mother's presence and himself as a loving being, the Buddha realized that the sense of being connected— of life's interdependence and relationality—is hardwired into our brains. We need to do nothing to establish it, though we often must clear away the obstructions that have obscured it. Epstein calls it "implicit relational knowing,"* and it is with us from the beginning, clouded though it may become by trauma and other life events. Implicit relational knowing is what accounts for our knowing how to get along with others, sometimes beyond what we might ever have been explicitly taught or learned. Stated another way, we are hurt by our relationships, but we are also healed by them, and we have that power inherently, as long as it isn't obscured by our own dissociations, addictions, or even ideologies!

Epstein's phrase—implicit relational knowing—provides an interest- ing and important counterbalance to Ian Suttie's notion of what is curative in the therapeutic experience. Suttie proposed that the curative moment in psychotherapy occurs when the patient finally trusts the therapist enough to reveal the source of their distress and symptoms: some "bad" feeling or an action that arose from it and the guilt and/or shame over it that alien- ated the client from himself and all others. The savvy therapist meets their patient in what Suttie calls a "fellowship of suffering"—a sympathetic reso- nance with negative feelings and experiences.[8]

Rather than touching on and admitting "badness," Epstein seems keen

---

* Sometimes, he calls it "intrinsic relational knowing." Epstein uses these terms interchangeably.

on reminding us of humanity's basic goodness, our innocence and sub-liminal "ethical know-how."* Rather than a discussion of the laboratory setting and particular parameters of a therapeutic encounter, he describes an exchange he has with a seminar participant, which begins with an anx-ious question from a man who describes the early loss of his father.

The seminar participant bravely recounts his feeling of deadness and lethargy, that life has been drained of meaning and value. This is all that is left, he says, as he sits with the anger he habitually feels when he thinks about his father leaving and his own irrationally blaming himself. Epstein offers an alternative path:

> By not fighting with his internal wounds, by not insisting on making them go away, by not recruiting everyone in his intimate life to save him from his feelings of abandonment, by simply resting with them the way we do in meditation, he could learn, as the Buddha did, that he already was the love he thought he lacked.[9]

That last phrase is so subtle it is easy to miss its import. Love is not something to "have" or possess or even to do, but to "be." Epstein encour-aged the recovering of—re-membering—the person the man was before his loss. In Epstein's version, recovery reminds the patient of his *goodness* and *love*. This is in rather stark contrast to Suttie, whose remedy consisted in assuring his patient that in her "badness" she was not alone and that the alienation that the feeling of "badness" caused could be overcome by the therapist's meeting her halfway with a general admission of his own humanity. Two sides of the same coin, perhaps? And Suttie *is* very keen on reframing humanity as basically good and loving, as making offerings of oneself as well as the therapist's love being key to the cure. In

---

* *Ethical Know-How* is the title of another of Francisco Varela's seminal works, which I highly commend.

Japanese cosmology, "original spirit" is that of health, a nice alternative to the conventional interpretation of the concept of "original sin." So maybe Epstein—and Suttie—are on to something in helping restore us to that self-understanding. And maybe it was this sensibility that so impressed my father and led him to affirm my "having made it out" of the oppressiveness of contemporary Christianity that, in a spontaneous moment, he revealed rather shamefully.

To assist in this recovery of our goodness and love and freedom, the broader form of the antidote is the holding environment that Epstein extols. As in the case of the Buddha, who was finally, at the point of his own enlightenment, ready to "make room for all of himself," the appropriate holding environment enables *not* dissociation but remembering. According to Stephen Greenblatt, this has been our mandate since Shakespeare penned Hamlet, though rarely, and certainly not culture-wide, followed. Nor, we may argue, has there been adequate provision for it, either theoretically or practically.

Re-membering, Dissociation, and Deep Communion

To clarify, Epstein makes the point a bit more graphically:

> Re-membering also connotes bringing that which is dissociated back into the self. It can mean rejoining, or becoming cognizant, in the sense of bringing something into consciousness that has been lurking outside awareness. In the case of trauma, this second meaning of remembering is especially relevant.[10]

As Greenblatt has taken pains to point out, revenge is to be replaced by remembering. As we saw in chapter 1, this wasn't easy for Hamlet, nor is it easy for us. It is natural to want to lash out and hurt someone when we've been hurt; Rosaldo's description of the headhunting tribe aptly illustrates this point. Or we react by engaging in manic economic activities, as the German psychoanalytic couple Alexander and Margarete Mitscher-lich document. In some parts of our own culture, we might argue that revenge—not to mention manic economic activity—is lamentably alive and well.

While a tradition of "manliness" and heroism may *seem* to be easier than the pain of remembrance, the mourner ultimately fails to find the dominance, status, or power they seek. The traditional route that skirts emotions also fails to gain the joy and bliss of companionship, collaboration, and co-creativity. In fact, aggression can be a symptom of the very trauma that needs healing—a holding environment that facilitates grief and resolution, a rejoining of a fragmented self.

D. W. Winnicott, a psychotherapist who did much to develop a method based on Suttie's work, observed that "if society is in danger, it is not because of man's aggressiveness, but because of the repression of personal aggressiveness in the individual."[11] To the extent that we suffer from a lack of social support for our grieving, we are, like the Buddha was himself, subject to dissociation and a seemingly endless spiritual quest. In a disso-ciated state, we are vulnerable to acting out, to uncontrollable urges and surges from places we don't even know exist—deep within our psyches and our lives—feelings we haven't had "held, verbalized, and understood." No wonder Mariah was anxious about "getting it right," and Sunny was anxious to know how best to support that!

Epstein's concept of implicit relational knowing doesn't require an elite education, wealth, or status—it is available to *all* of us, even if encrusted with our defenses and other responses to trauma, as was the case with the Buddha himself. Epstein reveals that early trauma was also the cause of his own disruptive acting out at one point.

The concept of implicit relational knowing provides a kind of natural, universal holding environment to facilitate actualizing the Buddha nature in each of us. This was especially true of the pilot program participants, the groups they formed, and the functions they fulfilled for each other. The only thing that *is* required of us in this implicit knowing is a *willingness* to be open to, curious about, and accepting of our dissociations—the parts of ourselves we don't want to acknowledge or affirm—in the work toward freeing ourselves toward "flow." This ultimate state of "flow" is being able to respond spontaneously appropriately in any and all circumstances. Since Epstein presumably knows nothing of hōji and kuyō, the extent of his recommendation of where to find such a holding environment is to try "one's partner, mentor, therapist, or journaling." My experience of these rites doesn't negate the potential helpfulness of or even, depending on the complexity of the grief, the need for the supplemental assistance from partners, mentors, and the like. But I have a hunch that the rituals provide unique elements that ground any support given and make it even *more* meaningful, profound, and mutually satisfying.

I believe that the Japanese have established in the rituals of hōji and kuyō the kind of holding environment Epstein commends, supported by culture-wide habits of humility, responsiveness, and reverence, as well as robust patterns and practices of interrelatedness. In my pilot project, we re-created the conditions of these rituals and succeeded in freeing participants from stuck places that had hung them up in their attempt to fully grieve their losses. Some of their stuck places may be similar to experiences you're having. It is my hope that knowing how the project participants worked through their blocks, their dissociations, may provide hints for where you might look for your own and tools for getting beyond them— allowing yourself to join, as they were able to do, in a less fettered flow of life. And equally importantly, for you to gather the insight, attitudes, and habits appropriate to supporting others in their grief and in their attempt to remove the blocks from their own participation in flow.

6

On Reverence:
The Cost of Its Absence

*Death calls us to be reverent together, but we often find ourselves
in groups that don't know how to do this.*

—PAUL WOODRUFF

Deepening our understanding of how to better process and respond to grief, we reach the topic of reverence, which I am ever more convinced is the main ingredient in grief—whether the grief in question is tending to our own, being helpful to someone close to us, or responding to the grief of the world constructively. Why might this be? What does reverence do for us? Let's take a look.

As with our discussion of the ego and what *it* does for us (or not!), and what a living Buddha is and is *not*, let's look first at what the *absence* of reverence costs us. My hope is that in discussing what reverence is *not* clears away the underbrush of misunderstandings and enables us to engage better with what reverence *is* as well as find our path to cultivating it.

The Absence of Reverence

Perhaps the most prevalent advice on the internet for friends of the bereaved pertains to "what not to say" to someone grieving—identifying the well-meaning but often subtly hurtful things that people say to others who are mourning. I recently saw yet another of these videos and, while some wisdom was offered, in my mind, it still fell far short of providing adequate advice and support. Why? The speaker failed to display an attitude of reverence when she suggested that we *should* say, "I am sorry for your loss." Now, why, you might ask, is that increasingly common phrase lacking in reverence or even considered offensive to some? Because it distances the person offering sympathy from the one who is grieving by subtly putting the loss solely on the mourner, without acknowledging that *her* loss is also *my* loss.

A more reverent attitude—one rooted in an awareness of the interdependent nature of all things—would stop at a deeply resonant "I'm so sorry" and leave it at that. I like what I've been told that families of Latinx heritage say, "I accompany you in your loss." But this statement in a WASPish context could be considered a bit presumptuous as is, I fear, and it would be a special situation in which I would personally feel comfortable saying that, however much it might be true or I'd *like* it to be true. I must admit, I have a kind of "holy envy" for Latinx culture because of what often appears to me to be their intrinsic warmth and habits of interrelatedness.*

That is just one example from a host of things we say to the bereaved that might not only fail in their purpose to comfort but could actually cause more pain. My assertion here: If reverence is properly cultivated, such incidents would become rare. And more *actual* support would be felt.

Remember Mariah's complaint of "hug rape"? I think prolific Irish author, expert in Celtic spirituality, and former Roman Catholic priest John O'Donohue captures the reason for Mariah's discomfort best. In

---

* "Holy envy" is a phrase coined by the late Krister Stendahl, former bishop of Stockholm. I heard him use it in an address to alumni at Harvard. Barbara Brown Taylor, a well-known Episcopal priest and author, has written a book by that title that elaborates on the idea.

his lovely exposition on beauty, he notices the way we frequently feel entitled, somewhat mindlessly, to barrel into someone's situation. He attributes this to a lack of reverence, which ultimately creates disappointing experiences.[1]

Aside from hugging an introvert who *really* would rather you not, another well-meaning area into which friends often barge in that turns out to be unwittingly oppressive is encouraging reconciliation with an estranged family member "before it's too late." That is, before the loved one dies and the survivor is left with regret and an unfulfilled potential *for* reconciliation. Granted, reconciling during the lives of both parties is ideal—providing more time and experience to take the place of the pained estrangement. Sometimes, though, situations are too complex to sort out in a short time frame. The Confucian tradition recognizes that resolving such difficult circumstances can often take generations. Jewish scholar Jon Levenson once noted that "the sins of the fathers" being visited on the sons and the sons of the sons for four generations is *not* a threat, but a promise: it *will* end. In the meantime, one might be tempted to obtain a "cheap grace," as the saying goes, rather than the real thing—a sincere and truthful reckoning with all of oneself and the behavior of the other and the cultivation of compassion for it all. These rituals and a proper understanding of their ultimate purpose open the possibility of cultivating compassion even beyond the grave.

Misdirected Reverence

Paul Woodruff, author of *Reverence: Renewing a Forgotten Virtue*, is keen to draw our attention to the possibility that reverence, even when present, can be disastrously misdirected, and even abused or exploited. Only fools and cowards show reverence toward tyrants, according to him. He is especially concerned about tyrannical parents who can take advantage of reverent children: "True homes are reverent, and their reverence restrains the abuse of power . . . Reverence hold men back from enjoying the liberty of wild animals."[2]

"Connection" Versus "Communion"

John O'Donohue, in addition to his concern with our irreverent approach to people and places, is wary, similar to Richard Fenn in chapter 1 and Wesley Carr in chapter 2, regarding our sense of time and the haste that we often embrace.[3] O'Donohue's positive appreciation for solitude and *taking* time to attend to our soul's longings make him a perfect resource for understanding the effectiveness of hōji and kuyō, the structure of taking time for grieving in Japan. He also offers a trenchant critique of connectivity as the goal of social life these days, something an early editor of mine was excited that my work might enhance. So I was particularly keen to understand his stance on this. Like Catherine LaCugna, a feminist theologian I cited in chapter 3, he prefers a deeper exchange with each other, something beyond the shallowness of social media, we might infer. If, as LaCugna has articulated, God wants the deepest communion with each of us possible, might it be the case that it is also what we want with each other?[4]

While valuing connection may have been a necessary first step in recovery from our tendency toward isolation and the hyperindividualism of our culture, it clearly isn't enough. The popularity contest that social media has become with the surface tallying of "likes" in the place of deep sharing is an obvious example. Recently, the surgeon general, who wrote a book on the dangers of isolation, has advocated putting a warning label on phones and other technologies that carry social media. I think of connection in terms of a train track: switching happens for us to connect to another track, but everything stays on the surface, with the possibility of derailment, collision, or the cartoonish rescue of "Nell" tied up to the tracks—or its tragic converse: the fatal failure in real situations when the conversation stays on the surface and never reveals or responds to actual distress. Compare with communion as it is traditionally understood in Christian ritual: the taking in deeply of the essence of another, which has been made possible by the self-giving of that other—the offering amounts to the giving of one's total self, not just a passing "like" or expressive emoji.

And the reason for our pushing toward connection rather than communion? It has to do with failing to access our own depth, to cultivate an awareness that arises from *there*. Like Francis Weller, author of *The Wild Edge of Sorrow*, who is concerned with our tendency to "amnesia and anesthesia," O'Donohue also points to the way we stifle ourselves, making our own deepest selves unavailable.[5]

This failure to access our own depths and the superficiality of our engagement with one another results in impoverished relationships, whether personal, political, or societal, and the consequences of a lack of communion can be dire.

Reverence Is Not Rigid or Humorless

For now, I want to continue with O'Donohue's observations a bit longer, in the hopes that they will help us recognize reverence when we see it and know how to cultivate it in turn. O'Donohue's Celtic spirituality—with its attunement to all of nature being imbued with spirit—aligns him with a similar, deeply engrained Japanese orientation to life and a source of the reverence one experiences so palpably there. Within that sensibility, I hasten to assure you that O'Donohue has no interest in sanctimoniousness or a rigid, contrived reverence, a put-on pretense. Even a "fake it till you make it" attitude would seem to offend. He affirms our playful nature and rescues it from being disparaged as irreverent. And, as I've always been taught, he asserts that humor is not the ability to tell a funny joke but the recognition of an appropriate perspective that allows us to laugh at ourselves.[6]

I'm *sure* this is true. On the rare occasions when my father and I sat in a church pew together in my formative years, he would lean forward and make the screws in the pew's wooden book rack *squeal* as he jammed a prayer book in behind a hymnal. He'd look at me with a twinkle in his eye, trying to get a playful co-conspiratorial rise out of me. Those are among the fondest memories I have of my father, for all their delinquency.

Of course, my second upbringing in Japan now precludes me from engaging in such antics myself, as that would be considered rude and disrespectful to the congregation and the priest. But I do deeply cherish my father's attempt to assure me that piety need not exclude playfulness and a sense of perspective—indeed, we must embrace it!

My most striking experience of this in Japan occurred while I was doing fieldwork at the first hospice founded there, located in Osaka. After a presentation I gave to the staff, a group of physicians and nurses took me to dinner. I was astonished at their sense of humor. But it made sense to me, their daily facing of death giving them a clear perspective on the folly of humankind and instilled in them an unusual capacity for robust, compassionate, and clean humor.

Reverence Is Not "Superior"

Finally, O'Donohue wants us to know that in reverence, there is no place for a holier-than-thou attitude or comportment, or capitulation to the idols of our day. He clarifies the frequently misunderstood relationship between humility and humiliation and shows that they are not one and the same. Rather, humiliating another, as in the case of slavery or rape, is a defiant and disrespectful failure to embrace one's humility, which ultimately leads to one's own humiliation. He is particularly concerned with our current state of acquisitiveness and how it contributes to our isolation and desperation—all a result of abandoning a sense of reverence.

What Reverence Is

So, what *is* reverence? I like Paul Woodruff's understanding, which combines high and low in a satisfying paradox, binding us together in our appreciation of the majesty and wonder of the universe (I'll get to his notion of awe in a bit) and *also* our aspirations after lofty things: "Reverence is a shared devotion to high ideals. Respect—the respect that flows from reverence—requires that we recognize each other's devotion to those ideals."[7]

Importantly, his definition doesn't end here. He also reveres—as do I—our struggle as limited, contingent human beings: "No matter how low, how immature, how foolish, or how weak in mind I think you are, reverence does not allow me to overlook our common humanity"[8] Critically, neither our commitment to high ideals nor our common humanity requires me to have a good opinion of you in order for me to treat you with reverence!

We have seen in chapter 5 how Ian Suttie embraces our common humanity in a therapeutic encounter, where he assures his patient that he, too, has been bad. And we've appreciated Suttie's approach to someone's utterance not simply as "self-expression," but as an "offering," with all of the sacredness that implies. I know that my own growth in reverence came about in large part due to realizing I was in awe of the creativity and perseverance of my fellow human beings in the face of unimaginable suffering and strain.

With respect to sharing ideals, Woodruff discusses the nature of an army and the principles that distinguish it from a gang of bandits—principles that inhere in the ideals and discipline it embraces. But there are myriad ideals we might be talking about as citizens, as fellow human beings outside of the context of an army assignment: the value of freedom, of truth, of love, of compassion, the pursuit of happiness, faith in God, an adherence to humanist principles, or respect for the scientific method, just to name a few. These ideals might be, while held in common, quite variously defined. I have a colleague who frequently finds himself in deep engagements with people on the other side of the political divide, and in those exchanges, he is able to constructively call into question their understanding of freedom and to suggest a whole new way of looking at it. His conversations are a prime example of the Confucian adage: "Put me in a room with any two people and I'll invariably have something to learn from them; from their good qualities, I'll take a model, and from their bad qualities, I'll take a warning."[9] I always learn from him, and I daresay his interlocutors must as well.

And before we stray too far from noting our current acquisitiveness as I mentioned at the end of the previous section of this chapter, I want to be clear that I do believe it is possible to shop—as George W. Bush admonished us to do from the National Cathedral in the wake of 9/11—in a state of grace or as a living Buddha. Here I take as my model thirteenth-century German mystic Meister Eckhart's Martha and Mary sermon. For those who need a refresher: Martha got upset at her sister, Mary, because she was sitting and listening to Jesus rather than helping prepare the meal. Eckhart offers, contrary to popular misconception, that it was Martha who was the mature spiritual being, able to both serve *and* be in mystical union with God. Eckhart was keen on the synthesis of contemplation and action, that is, the possibility of acting, indeed the imperative *to* act, from a state of union with God. And in Eckhart's interpretation, Jesus was assuring Martha that Mary would get there eventually! I am suggesting this as the source, for us in the West, of understanding what Keido was working to cultivate and what these ritual resources are ultimately geared toward doing.

Having outlined what reverence isn't and the dangers of its absence, I'll turn my attention more fully to what reverence *is* and how to go about cultivating it so that all our doings—and especially our mourning—have an adequate context in which to be conducted. And in the hopes of making the world even just a tad safer for our sorrow.

Cultivating Reverence

So, what gifts await us when we *do* cultivate reverence? When we *do* have an appropriate appreciation of the majesty, wonder, and suffering in the universe? A sense of perspective, good habits of humility, and an embrace of our interrelatedness?

First and foremost, perhaps, is Francis Weller's observation: "An approach of reverence offers us the chance to learn a more skillful pattern of relating with grief. When we come to our grief with reverence, we find ourselves in *right relationship* with sorrow, neither too far away nor too close."[10]

When I first returned to the United States from my decade-long sojourn in Japan, I was imbued with what I will call the personal atmosphere of reverence that results, I see now, from the rituals and resources

I'm commending here. My capacity for active listening was at an all-time high, and the riches that afforded me were palpable. That basic grounding in reverence meant that, once I began this work and was at parties where this became known, I was immediately inundated with fellow partygoers' stories of their own bereavements—as if the floodgates had opened and I were an ocean that could receive the flowing surplus and forceful waters of their pent-up feelings. I noticed this because it was noticeable to them: No one had inclined an ear to them in this way before; no one had been available to engage with them this deeply or on a heretofore taboo topic, though many might have enjoyed the "connection" that the party provided.

As I entered into the ordination process, I remember in particular the response a committee member gave to a question about me, that, unlike others going through the process at the time, I struck them as being "without an agenda." I wonder what Keido would make of that. It strikes *me* as being possibly what he taught, the state of mind he hoped would be cultivated by these rituals. As allowing one to respond "spontaneously appropriately to any and all circumstances" without being dominated by one's ego agenda and clobbering others with it.

As for what John O'Donohue sees as the richness afforded by reverence, he relates it to the ability to perceive to beauty, his main concern. And I believe it relates equally well to bliss and joy, that capacity and experience Mark Epstein suggests the Buddha rediscovered after it had been buried by an unmourned loss.[11]

Here, we finally begin to get to the heart of the matter: For Sunny, the key to helping her friend Mariah with grief is for Sunny to access her own depth, with reverence, and going from there. Cultivating reverence will ideally keep Sunny from unintentionally making hurtful, thoughtless comments because she will have an appropriate appreciation for the mystery of Mariah's experience, feelings, and future, growing out of the same respect for Sunny's own experience, feelings, and future. This deep respect that grows out of reverence will allow Sunny to provide the proper "holding environment" to let Mariah verbalize all her emotions and feel held and understood, which we all need and crave.

And in this space, Mariah will further be empowered to overcome whatever self- and other-loathing has crept in, as Suttie wrote about. Finally, and optimally, Mariah will see choices and know how to view herself *as* a living Buddha in her own right, capable of and overflowing with compassion—first of all, for herself. She can cultivate the depth that allows her to tolerate the high-voltage love like the Buddha's mother was unable to contain and the corresponding bliss and the tenderness to express this appropriately. A proper reverence will also allow Sunny to participate in Mariah's grieving through her own implicit relational knowing—accessing her own wisdom in spontaneous ways that truly support Mariah—because she's not responding in a cavalier, if well-meaning, attempt to cheer, cajole, or comfort. Together, they can wait for emotional catharsis, spiritual or psychological insight, and impetuses to action in the spirit of being led. They can see themselves as part of a common humanity instead of functioning out of a need for ego gratification, either as an ego-dominated participant in a hyperindividualized culture or from a combative, limited tribal allegiance.

Reverence and Humility

Perhaps I am stating the obvious here, but reverence has a profound relationship to humility—a kind of reciprocal and mutually reinforcing relationship. Humility makes reverence possible, and reverence reinforces humility. The pilot project participants exhibited humility implicitly with their willingness to seek help; to participate in an open-ended experiment with a few rules and guidelines established at the outset; and to offer their own experience, insights, and questions as we went along.

One of the most useful guidelines in cultivating humility is the strict observance of using only "*I*-statements." This is a standard group-process regulation, geared to warding off, or at least limiting, judgmental comments toward fellow group members, assertions of superiority, or attempts to "fix" the other. The nature of *I*-statements is to increase one's own vulnerability through self-disclosure, which simultaneously creates the conditions for deeper exchange than is possible in the midst of dismissive or derogatory remarks.

Participating in hōji and kuyō allows for our implicit relational knowing to be drawn out and contribute to the cultivation of reverence. Have you had the sense of "I don't know how I knew that, but I feel quite sure about this"? That is when you've accessed your intuition and perhaps observed something that could help someone. It is, of course, important to be humble about your pronouncements or observations.

Pilot program participant Jane was fond of reminding the group to "ask questions!" I take this suggestion and activity as the manifestation of Dan Siegel's basic "curiosity." An even kinder, gentler way of approaching someone to get their thoughts on a topic is to inquire, "I wonder what you think of . . . ?" or, "Have you given any thought to . . . ?" or, "What's been your experience with . . . , if you don't mind my asking?" One of my parishioners—a friend of Ruth's—once told me that when he was a member of the pastoral visiting committee and paid a call on someone, he would be very careful to make statements instead of asking questions—a variation on the theme of restricting oneself to making *I*-statements—as a way to avoid putting someone on the spot: "I enjoyed Rob's sermon last week, especially the point he made about . . ." or, "I was confused by _____ but have subsequently learned _____, which helped clear things up for me." He found that this made him vulnerable first and acted as conversation prompts.

Each week, I opened the pilot program session much the same way—with my reflections on something I'd said or done at the previous meeting that may have landed in a way I hadn't anticipated. This opened up the floor for a frank discussion about how the participants felt about it. This format gave them permission to admit to any negative feelings toward me, an authority figure, not necessarily easy to criticize or ask for an apology or clarification.

In their evaluations, I was pleased to see that the pilot project participants did often appreciate my facilitating, but also mentioned how helpful
the other members of the group were: implicit relational knowing at work!

Though I'd made the rule that participants humbly restrict themselves
to I-statements, as the facilitator, I sometimes made more "objective"
comments to normalize some of the participants' experiences—often
citing research that validated what a participant was reporting as common during grief. My aim was to help them overcome their sense of
isolation that is so pervasive in our culture's bereavement experience. I
suspect it also helped cultivate true humility instead of its false sister: the
holding back of an important perspective out of fear of offending someone or being seen as crazy.

A perfect illustration is when I highlighted Jane's experience of the flashing lights and gratuitous fire alarm at a church service, which she interpreted
as a sign from her deceased fireman husband, whom she was ready to more
fully let go of; Jane saw the production as his final greeting before ascending.

When I cited the research about Japanese widows having conversations
with the deceased and other paranormal experiences, and my vague recollection of another study that found these widows to be three and six times
healthier than American widows and British widows, respectively, Dave
had felt comfortable enough to chime in with his own experience of sensing the presence of the deceased: a visitation by his deceased grandmother
at the foot of his bed.

Reverence and Science

No one tried to explain away such phenomena, as we assigned them meaning and allowed ourselves to feel what those experiences generated in us.
Reverence doesn't deny that there may be neurological factors that pro-
duce such events, discernible by science. But it does provide science with
a larger arena in which to function—not as dismissing, reducing, denying,
or denigrating experience, but as allowing a depth dimension to undergird

and hold more warmly and compassionately, more imaginatively and humbly than what science alone can sometimes generate.

And yet, I don't want to be too quick to dismiss or denigrate science, either! Many priests in my father's generation came to the ministry out of their sense of awe at what physics was discovering. Science can provide occasions, in other words, for reverence just as significant and transformative as any more explicitly "religious" conversions. Take contemporary popular science educator Brian Greene, who has waxed eloquently about his own reverence as he views the cosmos from within his scientific profession. In a review of Greene's book, *Until the End of Time: Mind, Matter, and Our Search for Meaning in an Evolving Universe*, Dennis Overbye writes:

> One day, . . . he had . . . a sort of conversion to gratitude. Life and thought might occupy only a minute oasis in cosmic time, but, . . . "If you take that in fully, envisioning a future bereft of stars and planets and things that think your regard for our era can appreciate toward reverence."[12]

Reverence and Awe

For Paul Woodruff, cultivating reverence is about cultivating the right *feelings*, not just correct principles or proper thoughts, attitudes, postures, or lofty, otherworldly ideals. In his comparison of ancient Greek and Chinese Confucian cultures, Woodruff offers insight into the principles that undergird hōji and kuyō, which are rooted in Confucian culture. People are often surprised when I talk about how focused the Japanese *are* on feelings, as their signature politeness would seem to suggest anything *but*. So Woodruff's emphasis *on* feeling is a good guide for our grasp of the Japanese rituals of hōji and kuyō and how they work. According to Woodruff, reverence is the presence of three related feelings—awe, respect, and shame.

But also functionally, reverence is the combination of a sense of awe with knowing one's place in the world and the cosmos.

How, you may ask, is this achieved? And what do we mean by "one's place"? This will sound ominous to some who have been subjected to "knowing their place" as an act of subordination or oppression in the worst of ways. Of course, any human ritual can be abused in such a way. But let's set that aside for a moment to attend to the benign and even constructive meaning of "one's place." For even in our day, there is such an admonition to "stay in one's lane" as a reminder to mind one's own business. What is, then, one's lane?

In the rite of hōji in particular, a strict order is often observed in the offering of incense, an order that reinforces one's understanding of one's "place" in the world. As with my son's martial arts training, in which the student bowed first to the other students more senior than he and then to the students who entered practice after him, such ordering has the effect of generating both deference toward those who come before oneself and gentleness toward those who come after. Gentleness—a variation on Suttie's "tenderness," which he decried as taboo in the West—is highly prized in Japan, where observations of that quality are often accompanied by a loud affirmation: "*Yasashiiiii!*" And admonitions *to* it are equally frequent: "Be gentle!" A close equivalent might be, "Easy does it!" But the gap is instructive: I would maintain that "Easy does it!" advocates a pulling back from or easing off what is an active and strong, perhaps dominant forcefulness, whereas "Be gentle!" acknowledges the active principle *of* gentleness— that gentleness can be embraced and acted on for its own sake.

And gentleness can be actively cultivated in these rituals. In fact, it may be key to solving our epidemic of loneliness and isolation. Suttie observed tenderness to be, after all, "the very stuff of sociality."[13] The tenderness taboo that Suttie identifies as pervasive in the West seems to be lessening a bit, in my experience. But perhaps not yet enough. Maybe these rituals can help.

Similarly, in the Confucian tradition, shame is a valuable feeling, as it is the key to modesty, the cardinal virtue that underscores and allows for the flourishing of all the rest. This fits with my experience in Japan and explains why I've always felt that the recent emphasis on the value of awe is only half the story—as is the emphasis on the negative experience of shame; that is, it gets us only halfway to the attitude befitting a living Buddha. Awe, to my way of thinking, is a kind of passive response to the splendor of the universe, or even to our being moved by the grit shown by fellow human beings in the face of tremendous suffering. And shame can be about dominance or entitlement—neither of which is meant here.

Reverence, on the other hand, suggests a kind of humility in the face of mystery, with regard to the suffering entailed in living, and with respect to the bliss that is sometimes bestowed on us, often undeservedly but cherished, nonetheless. Compared to the passivity and self-contained experience of awe, reverence feels to me silently expressive of a kind of active receptivity and even a kind of reciprocity, if you will, that extends to all of humanity as well as to the grander scheme of the cosmos. I am picturing the moments when we fall to our knees out of gratitude, relief, and joy—a deep appreciation of majesty, wonder, and suffering—and the times we reach out to help our fellow human beings. Wouldn't you say that physical involvement bespeaks a bit more than mere awe? And that the urge to help our fellow human beings is a participation in the humility that we all share in the difficulty of getting by.

Perhaps the best example of the Confucian appreciation for the difficulty of getting by and the innate goodness that impels us to help one another resides in the famous anecdote of the child and the well, cited by Mencius, a later Confucian sage. According to Mencius, it is our natural tendency to rush to rescue a child who's fallen into a well. I particularly like the concluding corollary: that where that *isn't* the case, where we *don't* have the impulse to help, something must have gone wrong for *us* for a very long time to attenuate or erase that basic goodness. I especially value applying this in reverse: bringing our empathic imagination to bear in trying to assess what might have caused the suffering for an individual who is no longer good in that way.

Reverence, therefore, is not only an appreciation of mystery, but an active engagement with the world, one that is spontaneously appropriate but without ego agenda.

Reverence and Ceremony or Ritual

More than awe, then, and often including a physical response, reverence frequently entails what Woodruff calls "ceremony"—a translation of the Chinese Confucian notion of *li*. *Li* is often rendered as "ritual," and I find both translations have their place. According to Woodruff, "Ceremonious behavior is a sign of reverence . . . it also shows respect for other people—a kind of respect that can flow only from reverence."[14] It is this quality that I believe would inhibit the less-than-felicitous comments that many bereaved are subjected to by their well-meaning but insufficiently reverent friends!

Friends are, I want to make clear, not to blame. In this culture, as I outlined in chapter 1, we have been without adequate ceremony or ritual for a long time—lacking appropriate forms *for* the cultivation of reverence. Like Henry VIII, we have become convinced of our "sovereign authority"—the seed or fertilizer, perhaps, of our hyperindividualistic society: "What I want is what I want, to hell with you!" Despite all of this, some folks *do* evince an attitude I would say is reverent. Surely, the pilot project participants accorded me reverence due to my ordained station. And, as seasoned Episcopalians, they were well-versed in and appreciative of ritual, what we call in our tradition "liturgy." But perhaps there's a place or a need for more self-conscious and extensive cultivation of the quality of reverence in our lives beyond the confines or cultures of church-celebrated ceremony. After all, people claiming no religious affiliation these days outnumber those who do. So I am sensing that a secular culture-wide embrace of reverence as a key concept, right up there with freedom and responsibility, is past due.

The pilot project participants' experiences will offer some insight as to common ways that we avoid or interfere with cultivating our depths, along with some suggestions or resolutions to get beyond those blocks. I will turn to the Japanese Buddhist/Confucian wisdom literature for that tradition's prescriptions in a moment.

But first, let me finish my thought about ceremony and its necessity. Perhaps the best illustration of this is an episode in Ruth Ozeki's novel *A Tale for the Time Being*. A counterpoint to Keido's incident on the subway with the ruffian teenage boys, in Ozeki's novel, an elderly nun named Jiko and her great-granddaughter, the protagonist, Nao, come upon some rowdy teenage girls who are taunting them from a distance as they approach a convenience store to buy some snacks. Jiko approaches the girls (over Nao's frantic pleas to run the other way), stands before them, and bows the deep bow from the waist. This has the desired effect: The unruly girls draw themselves up and bow from the waist in response. The granddaughter simply stands there, stunned and not quite knowing what to do, and receives an elbow jab from Grandma to fall in line and join in this ceremony, this reverent ritual, which amuses the group of girls and further wins an appreciative giggle and their affection for the elderly nun.[15] This brief episode is another perfect illustration of the Confucian adage: Arrogance wins hatred; modesty wins love.

Respect Rooted in Reverence

The elderly nun Jiko is bowing to the Buddha nature in each of the girls, which has the salutary effect of activating that very nature. What a difference might it make if we greeted each other with a reverent bow, whether in personal, business, or even political relationships? Susan Cain, in her book *Bittersweet: How Sorrow and Longing Make Us Whole*, cites research on the prospects, noting that bowing "activates the vagus nerve" and contributes to a lessening of the sense of superiority that keeps us apart.[16]

It should be noted, though, that Woodruff warns against a strict adherence to form. Improvisation, he wants us to know, is not necessarily an irreverent thing by any means. In fact, I encouraged my pilot project participants to adapt the customs we were exploring and to report on those adaptations. I hoped this would help me understand what Americans needed to know and do to most effectively and accurately adopt these ritual resources. When I instructed the pilot project participants to consider building an altar where the deceased might be honored once or twice a day during our eight-week session, Katie and Charles's adaptations, in particular, illustrated implicit relational knowing and the respect they had for their partners.

A member of Katie's family was not terribly keen on her indulging her grief for her brother, who'd died just a year before. So as not to be "a stumbling block" to them, Katie discreetly placed the altar in her study, nestled in her professional bookshelves. And Charles went to yet another degree of consideration for his spouse and refrained from building an altar altogether. While his wife had been very encouraging in his decision to join our group to mourn the passing of his first love, Charles wisely allowed the "altar of his mind" (again, to quote Marianne Williamson) to suffice for his daily ablutions and then our group to be his witnesses and holding space for his reflections from the previous week. In both instances, neither seemed to suffer a lesser effectiveness for the sake of their social sensitivity and self-sacrificing, self-emptying mode of engaging in the practice.

I'm guessing that Woodruff's admonition against strict adherence to "social posturing" is what Keido meant when he corrected an assumption I had been making for years—that one can effortlessly, somewhat mindlessly, be "spiritual." We hadn't been speaking of this explicitly, but his noting that one must be intentional in one's spiritual life felt like an intuitively apt corrective to my "going through the motions," as it were. I went from sloppy and habitual in my social posturing, my mirroring the behavior without connecting it with my intention, to a gradually increasing degree of purpose and dedication, one might even say, devotion. Dare I say "reverence"?

This is where sincerity and truth come in. And where it pays to have removed one's dissociations so that one is free to be sincere and truthful rather than deflecting, disingenuous, or in denial. And one other piece of good news: In case you haven't surmised it in what I've said so far, let me assure you that there is nothing you need to do in cultivating reverence except to be sincere and truthful and give it time to *be* cultivated—to arise naturally, spontaneously in the context of your ritual undertakings. One need not, in other words, have been raised in a religious tradition or be "religious," or even be particularly reverent as one approaches the ritual activities: not exhibiting a false piety. Reverence *does* require an intentionality—*not* to "be" reverent, per se, but to be *open* to or *willing* for reverence to arise as well as participation in contexts and actions in which reverence is allowed, welcomed, embraced, and cultivated. And to do so often enough that reverence becomes the default position: like Jiko, the nun, who didn't think twice but just spontaneously and naturally approached the gangsta girls with the reflexive deep bow, which brought out the same in them. To the extent that one's dissociations get in the way of that is the degree to which it pays to work to remove them, or rather, heal the split in us that has brought the distress about. As we often say in the West, the truth will set you free, and in that freedom, reverence naturally arises.

How, now, we need to ask, can we cultivate the reverence we've described to the beneficent—even blissful—ends that Woodruff, O'Donohue, and Epstein invite us to? That is the subject of the next chapter.

7

Cultivating Reverence

n the previous chapter, we explored what happens when reverence is present, when it is missing, and what reverence is. In this chapter, I describe how reverence is cultivated and, in that, go deeper into the pilot project participants' experiences putting these rituals and understandings to the test in helping them with their experience of loss.

Reverence and Bowing

Woodruff is concerned with Confucian values and culture, not Buddhist (nor Christian), and so he doesn't cite the particular "ideal" of the Buddha nature (nor the Christian ideal of union with the godhead or the kenotic self-emptying example of Christ, for that matter). But reverence for the Buddha nature in everyone is the ideal that animates the Buddhist nun in Ozeki's novel. As I've noted at the end of the previous chapter, at a critical juncture, the nun bows to the Buddha nature within each and every one of the girls—girls whom her great-granddaughter fears may do them harm. The Buddha nature may be quite deeply buried within us but is alive and well, regardless of the outward, momentary bad behavior in which we may be engaged or garb in which we may be draped. And, sure enough, the active appreciation for the Buddha nature in the girls has the desired effect: They bow in acknowledgment of the nun and *her* Buddha nature.

I like Ozeki's imaginative episode also as an illustration of Woodruff's notion of the value of culturally established ceremony, as opposed to made-up, ad hoc ritual. The girls know to bow in response because bowing is a pervasive, culturally shared habit of humility in Japan. Woodruff points out that

> Ceremony is like a language: You cannot simply invent it and you cannot do it all by yourself; it must be part of the texture of a shared culture. You need not believe in God to be reverent, but to develop an occasion for reverence, you must share a culture with others, and this must support a degree of ceremony.[1]

At an international exposition organizing office in Osaka in the late 1980s, where I was working at the time, a foreign visitor to our office, a man from India who came with a briefcase filled with cash to secure an exhibition site, commented on how impressed he was with the Japanese custom of bowing. It moved him deeply, he said, and garnered his profound respect and admiration for Japan. I had become so accustomed to the gesture that I did it frequently, in modified versions, even after returning to the States in 1990. When I was leaving my first parish as a priest to go back to grad school, one of the women I'd worked with admonished me never to give up that habit. And Susan Cain, in her best-selling nonfiction book *Bittersweet*, advises her readers to "first, learn to bow."[2] It seems to me it has, in fact, started to become a pervasive custom here already. How tragic, though, that the football players who "took a knee" were so profoundly misunderstood by so many. Rather than defiling the game or the anthem or denigrating their country, they were, in my mind, pleading with us to live up to the ideals espoused by all of us (presumably). On one knee: Isn't that a posture of begging, as a courtier begs for his lady's hand in marriage? Can't we be wed to our ideals and each other as brothers? Isn't taking a knee, in fact, a gesture of *reverence*?

Woodruff explains how we might miss this meaning. Within a diminishing sense of reverence, in general, he observes: "What we are losing is a language of behavior—a self-conscious sort of ceremony—that best expresses reverence in daily life; and, along with self-conscious ceremony, we are losing many of the occasions on which people used to find ways to be reverent."[3]

I understand that some folks resented the disruption to the game that this represented to them. But given the loss of opportunities for this sentiment to be expressed, I empathize with the need the players felt to avail themselves of this chance to remind us of our ideals.

Reverence and Offering

In addition to bowing, there's one other element in hōji and kuyō that I find salient in cultivating a reciprocating reverence: the offering of incense and, in some instances, food and drink. With respect to the latter—offering food and drink—not all the pilot project participants shared my view or chose to make offerings of that nature. One participant even spoke rather dismissively about the offering as "quaint." And here we can begin to discuss dismissiveness as a sign of a kind of dissociation—perhaps a holding at arm's length the whole nature of nurturance, even. I was taken aback at this expression of disdain and didn't think to probe it further at the time. After all, everyone was free in our work to express their feelings without judgment. And it was part of my purpose to see how Americans responded to these resources. But this does not mean that all feelings are equal; to the contrary, some feelings and some ways of expressing them are indications of an unattended distress—such as Mark Epstein has identified that the Buddha himself suffered and learned to release. To be clear, I am not in any way suggesting that her choice *not* to make food offerings was wrong: She was free (as I explained in chapter 1) to engage with as little or as much as she wanted of these ritual elements. It was *how* she expressed herself in relation to her choice that seemed to disclose in an indirect way a dissociation.

In the case of this pilot project participant, I sensed the depth of the dissociation that might be prompting this, at a level not amenable to remedy in a public forum or with one simple or even potentially curative curiosity. One-on-one sessions with her did ratify my hunch that she'd been neglected in early childhood, and her scars from that beginning got in the way of her relationships more generally. That participant did go on to find another suitable offering—biblical readings and writing from other sources, a testimony to the essential nature of offering and the importance of participating in it in some fashion. It also speaks to the improvisation that these rites allow.

Offering as Nurture

A difficulty with nurturance in general is also quite common in our culture, I suspect. After all, if our attachment goals are *not* learning the give-and-take of mutual relatedness as it reportedly is in Japan, but rather the fostering of an independent and adventuresome spirit, as I discussed on pages 59–62 and 84–85, we may lack sufficient opportunities—I know I did—to become skilled in reciprocity, the kind of thing that this ritual banks on, cultivates, and engenders. For a time, my sense of deprivation in this vein made me positively desperate: I felt I hadn't been given the tools for living. *Where, as a young adult, could I garner them at this late date?* I wondered.

During my dissertation research, I met a Japanese woman at a ritual event in Japan, who had been similarly deprived. Her remediation came in the form of her marriage and being tutored, then, by her mother-in-law in these rituals and their attendant guiding wisdom, strengthening my perception of the salience of these rites in instilling and offering opportunity for nurture, even belatedly, and for practicing reciprocation and other virtues—even, and especially, self-love. Recall, if you will, Fenn's observation that "remembrance" is an opportunity, "a way of reconstituting the self; old love returns, and in its warmth the soul's own self-feeling is rekindled."[4] We might say, that's what happens under ideal conditions. Love is rekindled—for both the dead and oneself. But my hunch is that hōji and kuyō, if practiced appropriately, are at best—according to Keido—opportunities for self-love to be found and become the basis for compassion for all others—an experience of union with all of life. In Keido's estimation, and from his teaching that the purpose of the rites is not to make "dead Buddhas" of the deceased, but rather to make oneself a living Buddha, I don't think it's a stretch to say that offerings made are not for the dead at all! In other words, the dead are the occasion for but not the ultimate object of the offering.

If you find yourself identifying with this pilot project participant's dismissiveness, you might ask yourself how well you have been nurtured in your life, especially in your childhood, where early wounds, like the Buddha's own, can lurk in the background and leach our energy and openness to being led.

And even in strictly Western styles of grieving, Colin Murray Parkes—the British psychiatrist and researcher I mentioned in chapter 2—made much of issues with what is called "attachment"—the nature of the way we relate to our earliest caregivers—and its impact on the way we grieve—or are embattled in that effort.

I'm aware, too, that there is potential for this notion to be wounding to the reader. If you feel wounded, please notice that and be tender with yourself and others, remembering that hurt people often want to hurt others and, if lacking discipline—or a supportive social environment—will do so. An exercise of your empathic imagination, as Susan showed us in relation to her cousins, and as I described came over me at the birth of my son in relation to my grandmother, might yield a new understanding of the circumstances that deprived you of nurture to which you were entitled. And remember: The ultimate goal is compassion. But there is no rush to get there—an experience of all the feelings that may have gotten dissociated is the fastest route to it.

Riane Eisler, in her book *The Chalice and the Blade*, argues that Western culture has subordinated the value of nurture and growth—the feminine interests and capabilities—to a preoccupation with aggression, dominance, violence, and even war.[5] Does your own experience reflect this? Does your experience make it difficult to set aside the ego with its urge to dominance? Spending some time in a self-conscious effort at nurture can begin a healing process in this arena, as I myself have found

Suttie's work, valorizing the act of offering and seeing the improper fielding of it as the origin of hatred, seems relevant here. Have your offerings been poorly fielded? Has, for instance, your sharing of experience and especially of feelings elicited dismissiveness, disdain, or a redirect? How many times I've been in conversations where one person with a low tolerance for negative emotions has tried rather abruptly to change the subject! Or, worse, attempted a change of topic with a mocking putdown. ("Anything else, Cheerful?!" was a wife's attempt to get her Parkinson's-suffering husband to get off the subject of his current symptoms.) How might you have improvised to adapt? What kinds and degrees of hatred might you be harboring that drain your energy and make it difficult to experience bliss, to respond "spontaneously appropriately in any situation"? As Francis Weller has pointed out, joy cannot be experienced unless we are free to appropriately feel its opposite: sorrow. In a similar vein, love can best be experienced if the capacity for hate—for *feeling* it but not acting on it—is free to function: to be acknowledged, understood, and allowed eventually to be displaced by compassion.

My mother often gave the well-intentioned but ultimately unhelpful advice, "We don't hate—we dislike passionately!" But I'm afraid that only served to strengthen an isolating, fragmenting superiority in us, instead of a humble sense of our sharing in all of what it means to be human. I think it's far better to admit our hatred as a feeling that we *choose* to drive our compassion instead of acting on the hatred.

Reverence Requires Cultivating

Another stumbling block to effective engagement with these ritual resources and their accompanying reverence could be a person's fear that they don't have any reverence to begin with. This might have grown from a kind of shyness with respect to any inbred reverence or previous expo-sure to religious ritual a person might think these rites require. So if this describes you, here I offer some reassurance. One need not *have* reverence or *be* reverent to begin with, so don't let that stand in your way! As one of my colleagues is fond of saying, courage is not what you need to act; if you wait for courage, you may be waiting forever! Neither is courage fearless-ness. Courage is acting *despite the fear*. Courage is what arises in the midst of acting. Courage is *forged* in action.

So, too, with reverence: The point of the rites of hōji and kuyō is pri-marily the cultivating of reverence. Reverence, the Japanese have long grasped, is not an abstraction; it arises in and requires for its cultivating a concrete, *relational* context, since life *is* relationship. The Japanese have long embraced their implicit relational knowing and submitted to cultivating the proper conditions for the flourishing *of* relations by observing these rites.

Reverence for Healing

So, now we are prepared to more fully tackle the subject of dissociation—deflection, deferment, or denial of thoughts and feelings—and its influence on grieving. Reverence, we will see, forms not only the proper basis for respect, and the reserve that is helpful in relationships and particularly in the task of responding to a friend in grief, but reverence is also the basis for recovering parts of ourselves we have lost to this most basic defense against things we don't like—dissociation.

In my own life, not unlike the pilot project participant who disdained the act of offering at her improvised altar, my personality contained an undertow of defiance, derived from an early perception that my parents' preoccupations left too little room for me, so I would need to fend for myself. My preposterous resolve in that vein deprived me of much-needed help in the tasks of growing up, in much the same way that the historical Buddha lacked an environment that sufficiently acknowledged, accepted, and affirmed all his thoughts and feelings.

Mark Epstein's point in this understanding of the historical Buddha's experience was, in fact, not that it was unique, but rather that many, if not most, have suffered similar, primitive traumas as the Buddha. So I'm not trying to make myself out here as on the same level as the Buddha any more than you are—and you *are*.

I did try to reach out in my teens to two doctors to get help with the estrangement I was feeling from my parents—the first adult internist I had upon outgrowing my pediatrician, and my first ob/gyn. The latter was a very nice guy and a good friend of my parents who couldn't really imagine what the problem could be. The former took the offensive: "I know your cohort; you're all just bad apples!" Not very helpful. And he reinforced my feeling that I was in this alone—a crystallization or an unhelpful hardening of our hyperindividualized society.

My sojourn in Japan was the first time I really let my guard down, softened, and began to trust more fully, facilitated, I reckon, by the reverence of friends and their well-honed habit of accepting any and all expressions of feelings. The trust engendered by that holding environment was the basis of my willingness to explore my calling to the ministry. But it would be decades longer before I unwound the tension from my idolatrous notion of self-sufficiency and began healing the wounds my defiance had inflicted. As it had for Lizzie, a young, single gal mourning the death of her father in the second of my two pilot project groups, my little altar became my "safe place." By that, I mean it was an iconic representation of what I felt was missing all along—a place to experience my life itself as an offering, one that I needed to have properly fielded—to be heard, understood, and held. To be received reverentially—not because it was worthy of worship in itself, but because it emanated from the vast cosmos, itself deserving of reverence.

I had been deeply wounded, I learned in therapy, by my mother's spying on me at play, and when I realized it, aghast, and ran to push her furiously from the crack in my bedroom door, she laughed, which I experienced as her mocking me. It would have been far better for her to have quietly crept away and pondered the creativity she was witnessing in her heart with reverence. I was told I was shattered by that event, and I have come to see that is true. How often, in our irreverent culture, do we do what the Buddhist scriptures expressly prohibit: put someone else down by way of elevating ourselves? By asserting, in short, an ego agenda rather than supporting someone else's innocent and necessary ego strength? And when one's offerings are not properly fielded, how often do we allow the hatred that such experience engenders to rise and fall and flow away *without a need to act on it*? But also, equally importantly, without a need to push it down and out of awareness, to deny it consciously but thereby give it even more power and the possibility of erupting uncontrollably.

Articulating, holding, and understanding our feelings allows us to move beyond the ego that has been injured—but not until. In moving beyond one's ego agenda, one no longer needs to assert an injured ego, which only serves continually to stir up *more* pain by acting out one's distress.* Moving beyond this ego state, we can let go of habits we've accrued to cope with the pain—habits that ultimately get in the way of being led. This freedom is, in fact, essential to being led, to becoming a living Buddha, spontaneously responding appropriately in any situation.

Healing and Hatred

As I became more and more aware of the dynamics of hatred and healing, which grew in the time I spent in contemplation, I came to appreciate that the Dalai Lama spends four hours each day in meditation. Allowing a free-flowing awareness of the emotions stirred up by social contact—much of it very unpleasant in our current political environment—increasingly calls for careful attending to often negative emotions so they do not exert an outsized influence on our actions, often taking the form of debilitating self-loathing.

---

* For an imaginative rendering of this phenomenon, you might be interested in the work of contemporary spiritual teacher Eckhart Tolle, who describes his concept of the "pain body" in *The Power of Now* (Penguin Books, 1999), 36–46. I'm indebted to Vagdevi Meunier for bringing this concept to my attention.

The other pitfall that contemplation helps us avoid is projecting what we don't like about ourselves—the sources of our self-loathing—onto others. Recognizing and accepting our self-loathing or even our hatred of others so as *not* to act on it has a pithy permission in the Confucian tradition. "The profound person is able to both love and hate," reads the *Analects* 4:3.[6] And I daresay that includes self-hatred. We will return to this.

In the meantime, I want to notice, also, that Woodruff would approve of the kind of improvisation my pilot project participants demonstrated and I encouraged. As I mentioned earlier, reverence, in his book, does not preclude adaptation and updating, even if acts of reverence are originally part of a shared culture. I will also reiterate that my instructions to the pilot project participants expressly permitted this kind of adaptation, since the project was, in large part, to learn in what ways and for what reasons Americans might want or need to adapt these ritual forms. I hadn't read Epstein at the time, so I wasn't fully apprised of the possibility of dissociation affecting a participant's experience and, conversely, the opportunity for healing that discovering the dissociation could provide. My own previous attitude toward healing itself is a case in point: "healing, schmealing . . . who needs healing?" Boy, did I ever—and golly, this dismissiveness I now see as a dead giveaway. So to speak.

So, now I believe we're ready to think more carefully about the pilot project participants' experience—even the places in which they, like the historical Buddha, were slightly dissociated, unable to accept or integrate their experience because of some kind of investment in a particular way of being or seeing the world. And how our observances of kuyō and hōji helped.

Dissociations and Healing

If Mark Epstein is right about the historical Buddha and the dissociation he suffered around the death of his mother, I believe it's fair to say that as a culture, and despite many people's good work over decades in the area of bereavement, we are still a bit detached from—one might say "dissociated around"—the experience of loss, especially but not limited to, the experience of a death of a loved one.

I'm taking some liberties with the notion of dissociation. While in a strictly clinically psychological sense, it points to aspects of the self that one has disavowed—split off and relegated to one's unconscious as being undesirable aspects of the self—here, I'm going to talk about relationships the pilot project participants had with others that included a bit of distance or diffidence that had not been negotiated and rankled in some way. I also find them deserving of consideration under the topic of dissociation—and of being seen as healed as a result of their participation in kuyō and hōji resources. Jane's relationship with one of her sons is a prime example.

Jane and the Progressive/Fundamentalist Divide

As I mentioned in the introduction, pilot project participant Jane was well into her eighties when she signed up as a member of my first group of the pilot project, and over the years had learned a great deal of flexibility and receptivity that had served her well. Yet her commitment to progressive principles had hung her up in dealing with her more conservative offspring. You may recall that, when I asked her whether she'd discussed with her children her mystical experience of sensing the presence of her fireman husband in the flashing lights and errant fire alarm at the church service, she'd taken the question home as an assignment. Jane returned the next week with a startling report: She'd had the most wonderful conversation with her fundamentalist son! I'm quite sure that Keido, who had a fondness for covered bridges, would find in this episode a perfect example of the kind of bridge-building that is available through these rites—and in the process, a way of becoming a living Buddha.

Jane went on to adapt the use of an altar beyond the limited scope of bereavement but much along the lines of the Japanese implementation of this sacred space: as a locus of offerings of praise and thanksgiving for all the good things in her life—the birthdays of her children and grandchildren, graduation from college of a grandchild, and the like.

Jane also adapted my rules of engagement, which began with the offerings of participants to be couched in *I*-statements. These statements limit the possibility of "fixing" ("You should _____") or worse, accusations or blame ("You shouldn't have_____"), which create unhelpful resistance in the hearer and introduce a judgmentalism or even arrogant presumptuousness that is wholly unhelpful and has the potential to create hate instead of love, the love we're aiming to extend and expand upon in our ritual observances. But Jane rightfully saw the limitation of this approach and, in an adaptation of my opening remarks in each session, when I'd ask participants if something I'd offered in the previous session had landed in a way I hadn't intended—the unintended consequences that are always a present possibility in all our encounters—became enamored of and often preached herself the value of asking questions: "Have you thought of this-or-that possibility?" "What have you decided to do about this or that issue you raised?" and the like. This was a gentle and artful way to deepen the encounter, to take a conversation into areas many might want to avoid, but in a manner that allowed exploration of alternatives and a palpable experience of the richness of life and all its potential, overcoming together an often-subtle alienation or dissociation from self, other, and world.

She also coined an epigram for what was working best for her at her enlightened old age: AAA, which stood for acknowledge, accept, and affirm. This seems to me a brilliant summary of the very thing the historical Buddha discovered and promoted himself. One can only live fruitfully by accepting where one is and going from there. We have a tendency to make things worse for ourselves by layering unfulfilled expectations on top of our current experience. Another member of Jane's group and I discovered this when I saw that she was adding to her distress by expecting, as we often are led to in this still death-denying culture, *not* still to be mourning, though it was only six months since the death of her husband. I suggested she just allow herself to be where she was at the moment, which she later told me was a "eureka" moment for her and gave her great solace. Jane's AAA anchored her against such layering effect of unrealistic expectations and the dissociation from actual experience that entailed.

Finally, Jane fell in love again at the tender age of eighty-five with "a younger man" in his late seventies. Propitiously, this was on the one hundredth day of the pilot project, and so she generously attributed it to the work she'd done in it—freeing her from the burden of grief of two previous marriages—and the way it kept her from living life to the fullest—to live another day, love another way.

Susan and the Extension of Empathy

Susan's experience was similarly pliable, possibly aided by her training as a social worker and her great interest in the fruits of empathy and recognizing feelings, however obscure and hidden. So she grabbed hold in her little altar space and discovered her bias against overweight folks, which showed up in her disdain for her cousins, so endowed. This wouldn't do, she determined, and so she took a cue from my modeling of a gentle probing inquiry as to the struggles they endured and landed in a far better place, with overflowing compassion for them. Her disengagement from them in the form of a bias she harbored no longer formed a wall or dissociation in her life, which was far richer having discovered her capacity for compassion instead of her ego agenda of asserting her superiority.

Jenni and the Issue of Disloyalty

Jenni offered a bit more resistance initially, a sign of a bit of an ego tug-of-war, perhaps. As a reminder, Jenni had reported she had "only" had a conversation with her deceased father at her little altar space, and I had questioned the dismissive adjective. She went on to reveal her commitment—which she shared with her father, both being scientists—to the scientific method and a kind of rationality I'm going to characterize as "limiting." I feel I'm in good company, because it was part of Einstein's method to engage in "empathic imagination": It was how he first hypothesized his general theory of relativity, by imagining himself on a beam of light, how that might feel and what might occur as he traveled on it through space.

I offered this story to Jenni, along with the scientific studies of the superior health of Japanese widows who engaged in flights of fancy and dialogue with their deceased husbands, in comparison to their American and British counterparts. These scientific corroborations created an opening in her approach and freed her from her self-limiting convictions. In Jenni's final evaluation, she extolled the program for helping her overcome the blocks to her mourning. Other successes in her life illustrated even more profoundly the flow that she had entered and was enjoying.

As I've reflected on it since, Jenni's experience seems a variation on a very common theme in bereavement: a fear of disloyalty to the deceased, especially in acts that could be seen as "disloyal." To many in our culture, this is particularly pronounced because we don't observe an ongoing schedule of memorial events, so the threat of "forgetting" or *feeling* as though we are forgetting the deceased—and that as the disloyal act—is very real. A variation on *that* theme showed up even in Japan, where, during my dissertation research, I interviewed a widower in early middle age who'd become a sought-after bachelor getting pursued by eligible single women and/or prodded to consider remarrying even by friends of his late wife. This caused him all sorts of consternation as he struggled with feelings of disloyalty toward his wife, until I asked him directly what he imagined she would want for him. This was like a light bulb going on, apparently, as he realized and said aloud for the first time that of course she would want him to be happy, and that would include remarriage.

Charles and the Divide Wrought by Idealization

The tendency toward idealization of the deceased, which often occurs in bereavement, was illustrated as Charles mourned his first love, who had recently died. Charles shared with the group his passionate history with his first love and experienced the intrinsic relational knowing of his fellow project participants and their welcoming of his story with open arms, holding it with him. This reaction from the group had the desired effect: Charles felt safe enough despite his vulnerability to tell us of his disappointment when he'd gotten confirmation after her death that her love for him hadn't been as strong as his was for her. I'm sure it was painful: All disillusionment is! As prolific author Richard Rohr points out "the ego hates to lose—even to God!"[7] I'd like to think it was our holding the disappointment with him helped to cushion the blow.

Charles' experience is a great illustration of the process of idealization that is common in grief: Though he was a very accomplished, highly rational professional, it may strike you as a bit crazy to be holding on to such a love for so long a time. And, as we've noted before, people in bereavement often *feel* like they're going insane. *But* this is precisely the salience of grieving over time and opening oneself up to the painful discoveries that often await us in that work. It takes a brave man to allow himself the nurture we provided and his disillusionment of the idealized version he'd long held of someone dear to him!

Brian and Anticipatory Grief

Participant Brian began the program engaging in a bit of anticipatory grief in a scenario that is all too common but oft overlooked as a very real and significant source of grieving: for a pet. In Brian's case, his beloved dog. Vacillating in his worry over the dog's symptoms and the timing of putting her down, one day Brian copped to feeling like "an a-hole" for the frustration he was feeling and his wanting his wait to be over. No one in the group doubted Brian's love for his dog, so it was easy to empathize. Instead of attending our last session together, Brian used that time to lay his sweet pup to rest. It seemed to me that articulating even the feelings he was not proud of—that is, his ambivalence—helped him to more fully enter the flow he needed to carry him through the painful feeling of letting go he was facing. This allowed him to make a choice that was in the dog's best interests rather than as an overcompensatory measure of holding on to the ailing pup as a defense against his mixed feelings. Anticipatory grief can aid in just this way: identifying and articulating ambivalence to enable one to get beyond that oscillating mire and ultimately choose to be a living Buddha, full of compassion. In other words, resolving the ambivalence in the direction of compassion and its mandates, its flow. But anticipatory grief is not the only place where one can confront ambivalence; I daresay it is part and parcel of most, if not all, bereavements, since it is embedded in all of existence. And the reason we *need* to choose—why it comes down to choice!

Rickie and the Slavery of Resentment

And then there is Rickie, who vented to the group her harbored resentment toward her brother for the difference in care they provided for their parents. But in the end, she'd had enough of it herself and relinquished that grudge. I'm mindful of the phrase my uncle coined: "the slavery of resentment." Rickie seemed to believe it was time to set herself free and release her brother from the implicit judgment and superiority (prohibited by Buddhist doctrine, remember) to which she'd chained herself. I believe that the group was helpful to her process. Having been heard, understood, and held for a significant period—without judgment or pressure to forgive or forget or "move on"—it occurred quite naturally in its own time. Though we might also say, in our culture, it was anything *but* natural, but rather the effect of self-conscious, chosen intention on the part of *all* of us pulling together with her—being living Buddhas to her and with her and enabling, in the end, a wise and liberating choice.

Molly and the Group's Implicit Relational Knowing

Perhaps the most illustrative episode of the principle of implicit relational knowing occurred when one member disclosed at a session past the midpoint of the series of meetings that she was planning to go elsewhere for grief support. This was despite everyone having signed a pledge to do the entire eight weeks. I hadn't seen this coming, and an earlier self might have bridled at this rule-breaking. But my implicit relational knowing or the discipline to which I'd already submitted for decades at that point kicked in and, instead of taking it personally as an ego affront, I read it as the release of that coiled spring of aggression, albeit rather passive-aggressively expressed. And I sat back.

I—and I daresay, we—were all rewarded for my reserve, as the others in the group stepped up to express their sorrow at this member's decision to truncate her experience and deprive them of her input going forward—a perfect enactment of *their* implicit relational knowing and ability to get beyond their own ego agenda. In a less mature group, there may have been complaints of unfairness or looks to me for adjudication, even reprimand, for breaking the rules! A warm welcome was extended to this member for her return to the group upon completion of the other work. And I even managed to join in this generosity (much to my own surprise!).

In fact, that member did return for the last session or two that formed the initial series, and she also participated in the first anniversary meeting of the group as well as several individual sessions with me outside the group. We touched on the ambivalence that led to her initially leaving the group, though I'm not sure that it was ever completely resolved for her.

I am proud of the group, though, and pleased that we fielded her departure as the offering it was—with reverence and without judgment, with open arms and ongoing interest. I can be somewhat assured that our response, at least, was warm, open, curious, accepting, and reverent in such a way that we at least didn't *add* to whatever issues might have initially prompted her coiled spring to release itself in our group.

Molly's coiled spring release is reminiscent of my mother's goddaughter's outburst as we drove away from the gravesite of her biological mother, when she emitted a sharp, panicked cry while struggling to get out of the car to go back to the grave. She didn't want to leave her mother there. Luckily, her biological matriarchal grandmother had enough authority and intrinsic relational knowing that, turning around from the front seat, her firm "SHE'S NOT THERE!" settled the granddaughter with tough love and a reality check. The granddaughter was then able to go on to the dinner following the burial and participate meaningfully and satisfyingly, her anguish expressed in further feelings and soothing acceptance by other members of the family. (Another one I particularly recall was the daughter's sadness that her mother would not be alive when the daughter got married, sometime in the undetermined future.)

While this kind of constructive engagement *does* go on in our culture, we still need more work to get beyond the ego agenda of shopping and other addictions, the distractions of superficial engagements everywhere, of toxic positivity, of our "rush to the resurrection." But I remain convinced that there is much to be mined in attending to the primitive agonies* we may have accumulated along life's way. Bliss to be recovered, events in which to participate, fluid personalities wanting to evolve and be fulfilled, relationships aching to flourish.

Grieving can be a medium by which we achieve these depths, this richness of communication, communion, and community. It helps to have a framework and a few ground rules for guidance and practices that help us cultivate an appropriate responsiveness, reciprocity, and reverence. The Japanese understand that submitting to such a discipline is not an impoverishment but rather a route to becoming an adept, skillful person and a mature participant in a mutually gratifying society where relationships are understood to be key to life satisfaction. Appropriate responsiveness, as Ian Suttie has theorized, helps stave off an inordinate amount of hatred that arises when one's offerings are improperly fielded. Japanese attachment goals focus on fostering such a responsible responsiveness in the service of unfettered relatedness and flow. Observing hōji and kuyō continues the development of a rich inner life and gracious social interactions.

No matter what level or degree you choose to engage with these ritual

---

* This is D. W. Winnicott's term, quoted in Mark Epstein, *The Trauma of Everyday Life*, 29.

resources, I hope you will be gentle with yourself and others, even when situations may call for a bit of firmness in the form of reality-testing and tough love. That you will find what you need and revel in the discoveries they enable. That your thirst for revenge may be transformed by a disciplined, full remembrance, and in that, your emptiness will be filled with compassion.

Loyalty, Dreams, and Legacies

There are other issues that arise in the course of mourning that can be helped by observing these rites, either alone in the form of kuyō or with others on a sporadic basis with a larger social component. Loyalty, in particular, is difficult for many: We fear forgetting the deceased and being plagued by guilt for so doing; enter kuyō with its daily or monthly rhythms that are minimally intrusive but offer the sure knowledge and tangible action that one is *not* forgetting the dearly departed and, further, rekindle the love between the living and the dead through caring action.

Dreams can be as much the object of grief as the loss of any person, the German psychoanalysts Alexander and Margarete Mitscherlich showed in their analysis of post–WWII Germany entitled *The Inability to Mourn*. The German people, in their example, had to relinquish the dream of being led by a charismatic man and all the identity and ego agenda as well as ego strength bound up in that. But more modest, personal dreams are also achingly released in the course of mourning—and in time, replaced by new ambitions and aims. The time this can take varies widely, but marking the time with kuyō and hōji provides opportunities for developing new visions and articulating just what was lost—what *were* the dreams the deceased held with the survivors that are important to articulate, hold, and understand? Perhaps in that process will be hints of lessons to be applied in the next relationship or in one's life more generally or, conversely, the realization of completely idiosyncratic ideals or gifts that cannot, in fact, be replicated but can and should be honored.

One pilot project participant died after the project ended. I worked with her husband to ascertain what he valued as the legacy of their marriage and what he learned through it that he wants to do differently in his next marriage. Having help with this makes the whole process more bearable and broad-minded. In Mariah's case, for example, giving up on enjoying the vibrant presence of her sister was very hard—a giftedness Mariah could not duplicate but eventually yielded to an opening for Mariah to be more herself without somehow feeling she was second fiddle to her sister or sitting by in her shadow.

In all, the presence of others with whom one can safely express feelings and be held and understood provides myriad benefits: a diffusion of the burden of memories, gaining perspective by hearing others' interpretations or experiences, avoiding the sense of disloyalty when life continues without the deceased but there's no space for ongoing honoring of the effects of their lives on ours . . . of their legacy. Joining with others to share our grief also resulted in the recycling of hard-won wisdom by sharing one's gains in understanding with others who are struggling.

I do need to remind you that it is not just any context, nor does anything go, when creating opportunities to honor the deceased and share memories of the life shared. Certain ground rules and self-discipline help keep these gatherings constructive. Allow me to mention again the value and power of *I*-statements in creating the most appropriate context for conversation—one that will refrain from judgment and offer one's own experience as a starting point and invitation to a deeper dialogue where feelings may be heard, understood, and held. And where reality testing, apology, and gentle questions can be helpful and most welcome. Recall, too, that how you respond to what someone offers is important: that offerings poorly fielded can generate hate in the one whose offering is not well received. And know responding in a nonverbal way that reflects a depth of empathic resonance and reverence can be much better than a verbal bumbling about to find words where none exist.

And now let's look closer at how you can engage with the ritual resources I've described—from solitary, individual observances of kuyō to communal rites known as hōji as a simple structure or framework. Both can help us keep the oscillating that grieving entails within manageable bounds. These rituals give us reassurance that we are not forgetting our beloved departed, and in so doing, being disloyal. They provide us context for experiencing flow as living Buddhas who practice compassion and can respond appropriately in any situation, and for achieving depth of communication with others and communion with all things.

8

A Way Forward:
Implementing These Resources

As we've seen so far in this book, Americans, in particular, lack social structures or frameworks for the kind of support that has been proven effective—necessary, even—for successfully navigating the death of a loved one. Now that we've seen how kuyō and hōji have worked for a handful of Americans right here in the United States—frameworks that the Japanese have observed with notable positive effects—I want to outline how you, too, can pursue a practice—bereavement, spiritual, or both—that incorporates these ritual resources.

I'll start with kuyō—the individual practice you can do once or twice a day—since it all comes down to us as individuals and our choices, even as we work with and value the relationships in our lives. After a review of the practice of kuyō, I'll move into a set of suggestions for the use of hōji—the public rites and their syncopated pace, for use in families large and small. Finally, I make some preliminary recommendations for community adaptation of these rituals for consideration by churches and other faith-based gatherings, as well as nonreligious public institutions such as prisons, fire stations, community centers, and municipalities hard hit by devastating public losses, like New York City after 9/11 or Uvalde, Texas, after a school shooting in June 2022.

Kuyō: An Individual Ritual

For the Recently Bereaved

This rite may be conducted once or twice daily, at an altar you fashion at a designated spot in your home or at the "altar of your mind," again, to quote Marianne Williamson. Consider making an offering of food and drink, prayer, a reading or readings, and the use of candles and incense. Try to do it mindfully—aware of your thoughts and feelings as they arise without judgment and allowing enough time for your emotional state to reach some kind of equilibrium before you leave the designated space of your altar and the time you've set aside for this. You can come back to it: later that same day or the next day, for the first forty-nine or one hundred days—whichever schedule you set for yourself. Once the official period of mourning is past, make a special observance on the monthly anniversary of the death (say, if the death occurred on the seventh of the month, the seventh day of each month).

If friends or family come to your home in the initial period following the death, invite them to offer a prayer or simply their presence at the altar. Visiting with them in the proximity of the altar will remind them of the sanctity of the moment and your experience and invite them to share reverently in that sacredness.

If you are the chief mourner, consider inviting a priest, minister, or other spiritual teacher to attend once a week for the first seven weeks, and again on the one hundredth day.

For Ongoing Mourning

Past the one hundredth day, in addition to the monthly observances mentioned earlier, offer special remembrances of this departed loved one on the first and second anniversaries of the death and on the days of the extended schedule when the public rites (hōji) are not being observed.

Consider seasonal observances such as the equinoxes and solstices, New Year's, and Obon (mid-August).

Keep a calendar at the altar of the deceased members of your family to be prompted to acknowledge or be comforted by the recognition of the anniversaries related to them.

As an Individual Spiritual Practice

Remember the historical Buddha's observation: that there is no self without relationships; nature is inherently "relational." So a practice centered on the goal of becoming a living Buddha, as Keido instructed, does well to avail itself of the format of kuyō with its built-in acknowledgment of relationships and loss, reverence and relinquishing our ego agenda, even in the midst of allowing them to become conscious in order to give us a choice— whether or not to pursue our egoic drives or to cultivate compassion—for self, for others, for all things.

It helps to embrace a spirit of pilgrimage in approaching this spiritual practice: an openness to discovery, or, as neuropsychiatrist Dan Siegel encourages us, an attitude of curiosity (combined with openness, acceptance, and love; his acronym for easy reference is COAL). It was my dear friend and mentor, the very gifted and gracious theologian and minister Richard Niebuhr, who made me aware of this in a very appropriate setting: the last time I saw him alive. While I was there, Dick occupied the oldest chair at Harvard, and I benefited greatly from his championing of the work I was trying to do. In addition, he was the nephew of the famous theologian Reinhold Niebuhr, whom readers may recognize as the author of *The Serenity Prayer*, the backbone of twelve-step programs with its encouragement to change what can be changed, accept what cannot, and grow in wisdom to know the difference. My mother's uncle, Bishop Will Scarlett (Episcopal Bishop of St. Louis, 1930–1950), was Reinie's best friend, and so Dick and I had an ancestral tie along with our mutual intellectual and cultural interests. His father was H. Richard Niebuhr, a theologian and sociologist of religion. Dick created the Committee on the Study of Religion at Harvard University, which brought the opportunity to study religion to undergraduates as well as divinity school students in graduate degree programs, and was a great privilege to teach with Dick during my doctoral studies.

In my last encounter with him, Dick was in hospice, and I was urged by a staff member to read his own work out loud to him, which he was taking pleasure lately in revisiting. I was only too happy to oblige. The text I chose was his Parabola article on pilgrimage. When I finished reading it, I asked him if I could tell him what my experience of reading it to him was. Dick was nothing if not a proponent of the value of personal experience, so he was open, welcoming, and interested. I began somewhat tentatively, but in truth, emboldened by the very article I had just read to him: "When I started reading, I was aware of fearing your death, my fear of losing you; but as I kept reading, I came to understand that the point of living is to become one with all things, and I imagined you were reviewing your life and savoring each bit with that end in mind: to become one with it all. And this brought me enormous peace. I am no longer afraid of losing you."[1] In Dick's typically receptive mentoring, he sat back looking rather amazed, and said, through his still palpable aphasia, "I've never thought of it that way!" And he, too, looked relieved. It was a moment of mutual benediction and blessing. I will never forget it.

It is a bit harder to apply the ultimate goal and practice of becoming one with all things to myself, but I'm getting better at it. If the proximate goal is to learn to be led, then savoring each moment as an act of reverence and spontaneously right behavior is half, if not the whole, battle.

My encounter with Dick while he was still alive and its affirmation of that goal—becoming one with all things—ironically strengthened my conviction that this is possible to achieve even *after* a loved one has died.

I wish I'd known this sooner—I wish I'd had that encounter with Dick in which I became practiced in speaking my fear, talking about someone's

impending death with them—before then. I might have spared my cousin's agony over his mother's parting if I could have encouraged him with
this example then, which I hadn't at my disposal at the time. But sharing this story of my encounter with Dick with my cousin since then has
affirmed my sense that my practice—this practice—emboldens one, while
staying within the bounds of reverence, to speak of difficult things, including the impending death of one we love. I am lucky that way; I've been
lucky that way for some time. And I want to impart that luck to you. To
encourage you to find the ways to communicate—not simply connect, but
get to the deepest communion possible, as what God wants with us, for us,
and between us. It is worth it.

Hōji: For Families of the Bereaved

If you are so lucky as to have an intact family (more or less!), you might
want to gather them at discrete intervals for sporadic memorial observances
known as hōji. The first rite in the Buddhist schedule of observances is, in
fact, within the first year after the death: on the forty-ninth day and the one
hundredth day after the death. Savvy readers might recognize that these
intervals correspond with Pentecost in the Christian tradition, when the
Holy Spirit was sent to the disciples as long-awaited comfort in the aftermath
of the death of Jesus on the fiftieth day since his death, and the duration of
Kaddish in the Jewish tradition, lasting one hundred days.

Hōji may be conducted wherever the family or related folks gather,
such as in the home of the chief mourner (eldest son or widow, in the Japanese case) or at the temple or other religious institution where the family
typically worships. If at home, consider having a priest, minister, rabbi, or
other official come to conduct the ritual. This is not for the purposes of
proselytizing or imposing dogma, but could be helpful for steering clear
of misunderstandings and misinterpretations of religious or spiritual concepts. Mostly, though, the presence of an outside officiant can be rather
for the sake of the family members who are thereby relieved of the details

entailed in carrying off a ceremonial event and can therefore more fully participate in the emotional exchanges and release afforded by the occasion—can more fully grieve, in a word. The relative emotional distance of an outside participant can also provide perspective through a homily or eulogy, which can be very valuable.

If it is a funeral, the *Book of Common Prayer* includes a boilerplate office (service) that can be adapted for your purposes and also for a series of memorial events. It begins with words of setting the intention and mood and theological understanding of the event and continues with readings from scripture to provide solace and context and prayers for both the deceased and the mourners. In mainline denominations, where appropriate, a celebration of the Eucharist or Mass may also take place.

If appropriate, members of the congregation (the grieving family and friends of the deceased) may want to come to the altar to offer incense. In some instances, a tray with incense to be offered might be passed around to attendees in their seats.

If offering incense individually, consider whether or not you want to observe some kind of ordering of seniority to help reinforce both respect for elders and kindness to the junior members of the family.

The schedule of observances is uneven: In addition to the hōji conducted on the forty-ninth and one hundredth days after the death, hōji typically take place on the first- and the second-year anniversaries, then on the sixth, twelfth, sixteenth, twenty-second, twenty-fourth or twenty-sixth, the thirty-second, and fiftieth anniversaries, and then every fifty years thereafter, with lots of fallow time between ritual events. This gives you plenty of opportunity to do the work of mourning, emotional and practical, and make optimal use of the presence of others when you do come together at hōji events to find help with both those tasks. Remember, when processing your feelings with regard to how you feel about others, to ask yourself, "When have I behaved similarly" (in the case of a negative response to someone), or, "How can I incorporate more of that [kindness, generosity, attentiveness, etc.—positive attributes you admire in another] in my life?" As you may recall, the Confucian *Analects* recommends that "when in a room with any two people," you take a warning from their negative qualities and a model from their positive ones. A warning can itself mean many things, but in the "self-cultivating" interests of the Confucian tradition, one is encouraged to look for the evil within to avail oneself of an opportunity for self-correction rather than projecting our bad qualities on others or blaming them for our experience.

Remember, also, when confronted with a hardened sort, one whose first impulse on encountering you is *not* empathic and helpful, that something must have been going wrong for that individual for a long time to reach such a state of distress and disrespect. See if you can't engage—even if only in retrospect and the privacy of your own spiritual discipline—in some empathic imagination, trying to fathom the difficulties that person may be bearing. Is there a way you could ease some of that pain? For an example of how we handled this sort of breach of etiquette or rules, see my description in chapter 7, pages 154–155.

And always have at the ready an apology should you discover an infraction you yourself committed. Modesty wins love, remember, and arrogance breeds hatred. Try on the view that every life is an offering, that fielding that offering properly or poorly has profound implications, and that bowing as an act of reverence or appreciation for the mystery of that person's experience can set an encounter on the right footing or reestablish a footing gone wrong. For more on this, you may wish to revisit chapter 2, pages 63–66.

For Communities

As Bereavement Care

It's easiest to prescribe these customs or rituals for faith communities, since they originated in temples and shrines in the Far East. But it could be interesting to adapt these resources for use in communities such as retirement homes, fire stations, prisons, community centers—you name it—any place where losses occur and could be memorialized to the benefit of residents, employees, and staff. Famous physicist Brian Greene's appreciation—even reverence—for the cosmos reminds us that such an orientation to life is not necessarily dependent on having or belonging to a particular faith tradition, or any religion, for that matter (no pun intended). Observing these rites can redound to the benefit of everything from simply overcoming the denial of death to experiencing and expressing the surplus and force of emotion that attends grief to garnering perspective and help in recalibrating the pragmatic details of life going forward; did I mention cultivating reverence and the depth of communication and community that they would promote? The possibilities are endless in the ways we might make use of these rituals.

Since one of the greatest fears the bereaved face is the prospect of forgetting the deceased, I would start by compiling a calendar of losses in your community. This would enable an officiant or official at any given religious service or community function to have a ready reference from which to call out the names of those persons whose death anniversary falls on that day. Leave the calendar on the altar or another prominent and protected place to signal to the community as a whole the importance of honoring those who have gone before us. One church I know of constructed a wooden display case with a glass cover that could comfortably hold a large calendar turned to the day and containing the names of the deceased; they situated it in a corridor just off the main worship space with a fair amount of traffic.

Designate a member of the staff or trained volunteers to visit bereaved members of the community weekly after a loss until the forty-ninth day or at other intervals of your choosing. Many churches, for instance, have a pastoral care committee comprised of one clergy member to provide oversight and the rest lay volunteers from the parish, who make house calls under the supervision of the cleric. Perhaps municipalities could hire trained staff to visit the bereaved; it need not be a denominational or even religious thing, per se. Or an all-volunteer organization, such as Cruse Bereavement Care in the United Kingdom, which provides training for and then the actual visitations and other support services to the bereaved, could be established in your local community.

Make the facilities—a church, a community center, or other space—available for families to use for the purpose of family-based hōjis, and consider whether you, as a community, want to create a schedule of public events specifically dedicated to mourning the recently deceased or those experiencing any other kind of loss—divorce, unemployment, dropping out of school, and so on.

Consider creating a committee to provide refreshments or other hospitality after a hōji.

In convening for a public rite, keep in mind the pointers described for the family observances mentioned earlier. This includes:

- pragmatic planning, such as the sporadically paced ritual schedule and emphasis on emotion over form;
- structural elements that help participants feel a sense of their "place" and show both deference and kindness to fellow attendees and reinforce reciprocity and responsibility (such as an order for offering incense that reflects the communities' values, including hierarchies[*] and etiquette); and
- emotional tips, such as remembering to reflect on interactions with an eye to compassion, self-cultivation, and care.

For tailoring these rituals and customs to your particular community, jump-starting your observances by conducting the rites *in situ* for a time, or for guidance on specific situations that arise in your community, contact The Rite Source via email at mizutsu@theritesource.org, with the subject line: "Ritual planning help" or "Community issue" to discuss your needs and how we might assist.

---

[*] The Confucian tradition acknowledges "natural hierarchies" such as age or seniority, ability that creates experts, etc. Ideally, this is not rigid but relies on the kind of reverence and reciprocity I've tried to describe and prescribe, so there is no oppression involved but merely a mutual recognition and appreciation that creates reliability and relaxation.

As Spiritual Practice

Consider forming a group of contemplative practice for members of the community—church, retirement home, fire station, or other—who want the structure and companionship of contemplating together. Create opportunities—small group experiences, either as part of, or entirely separate from, or both the contemplation mentioned earlier—for members of the community to share their experiences with and insights gained or questions they'd like help with from observing these rites. Don't forget basic group best practices: using *I*-statements, respecting confidentiality, refraining from judgments (of yourself or anyone else's offerings), doing reality-testing, asking respectful questions, and having apologies at the ready as etiquette to be embraced.

I hope that, by this basic outline, I have shown that the rites of hōji and kuyō are adaptable to a number of settings. Their origin in Asian spiritual practices, with an emphasis on self-cultivation, compassion, and ethical know-how and *not* dependent on a so-called faith tradition with prescribed "beliefs" requiring cognitive assent, allows them to be incorporated into existing faith traditions or function in stand-alone situations where memorializing and remembering can be a constructive, community-building activity. The values that these ritual resources embody can highlight, resuscitate, and even rehabilitate values in existing Western faith traditions that have lain dormant or become distorted through disuse, misuse, or misunderstanding. Where no specific faith tradition exists or is mandated, a simple innate reverence or one inspired by nature and/or science can suffice to serve as the backdrop to or an adequate orientation for conducting the rites. It is my hunch that observing these rituals will cultivate a reverence not dependent on any faith orientation but foundational and functional for sustaining the best of ourselves, of each other, and of our culture. And, in the end, for making the world safe for sorrow.

9

For Research, Reflection, and Collaboration

t's my chief concern, my working hypothesis, and my growing conviction that I am not alone in having felt so desperately alone, and that the ritual resources of hōji and kuyō are invaluable in reconnecting us with ourselves, our social surroundings, and even the cosmos.

I've tried to do a "once over lightly" description of these rites I've known as well as the benefits to be gained by observing them, both as an aid to bereavement and as a more general spiritual discipline. I've attempted to get into the weeds just enough to ground this practice in a working knowledge of the essentials for its effective engagement. But there is much more to be explored and better described, fleshed out and understood. For instance:

- How might the practice of hōji and kuyō or adapted forms of them—and particularly the cultivation of reverence—contribute to curing anxiety and depression, countering loneliness, and slowing cognitive decline?

- How could the practice of hōji and kuyō or adapted forms of them form a more culture-wide hope, similar to the hope Dave gave voice to from his experience of the pilot project as it contrasted with the fear instilled in him in his upbringing and particularly through punitive notions of heaven and hell?

- How could the practice of hōji and kuyō bind together the generations as well as build bridges across political divides? Jane experienced such in her groundbreaking, bridge-building conversation with her son even though their differences in political opinion had formed a burdensome barrier. These were overcome through the experiences she shared with him of these ritual resources.

- How could the practice of hōji and kuyō or adapted forms of them transmit the legacy of families, as several of the pilot project participants noted happened for them? I am mindful of how often (always?) the people featured on the PBS program *Finding Your Roots* exclaim, "I didn't know *any* of this!" Well, here's a potential remedy for that failing.

- How might the practice of hōji and kuyō or adapted forms of them help in curbing crime, and especially the violent or exploitative abuses of our fellow human beings? How much of crime, violence, and exploitation takes place as a result of unmourned losses and the surplus and force of emotion that goes unattended? Would a culture-wide reordering of our values to focus on nurture and collaboration instead of dominance and competition, along with a better pattern of reverently acknowledging of our fellow human beings' various attempts at "offerings" help curb a tendency toward violent acting out? How might we create a new political reality by seeing that we sometimes allow our fellow citizens' offerings to go awry by failing to respond or by responding inadequately or by responding with disdain or judgment, rather than an attempt to understand? How could rampant hatred be calmed by a better "fielding" of such offerings and a response that fosters radical love instead?

- How might the practice of hōji and kuyō or adapted forms of them provide remedial opportunities for self-nurture? Might they help uncover areas in which we were insufficiently nurtured and, attending to the wounds of that neglect, assist in redirecting entitlement sensibilities from distorted demands to realistically providing for ourselves and others and ultimately cure an epidemic of frustrated narcissism?

- How might a fuller understanding of Christian precepts or doctrine, especially a Trinitarian theology rooted in relationality, help us make the most of the opportunity afforded by and through these rites?

- When horrific incidents like the mass shooting at Uvalde take place, how can we make a systemic analysis of what went wrong and place a greater emphasis on *relationship* and not the isolating, hyperindividual-blaming prescriptions for "better mental health care"?

- How can the practice of hōji and kuyō help us to redefine diagnostic criteria and mental illnesses as well as create better cures?

- And how might the discipline at the heart of the practice of hōji and kuyō help us be better friends, a key to the satisfaction available in this life?

- How might a culture-wide observance of these rites help offset the tendencies to scapegoating as Carrie suffered?

- What does grief look like when attended by these ritual resources? How does grief theory get ratified, revised, or embellished by this practice?

- What kind of society can we become by following these customs of memorializing and social support? Can our practice of these rites help us overcome the dominating tendencies of patriarchy and individual ego—toward a more collaborative, co-creative, and nurturing civilization not run by the military-industrial complex, Big Pharma, or the medical/insurance industry, but centered instead on creativity and growth, nurture and collaboration, determination and dedication?

Participating in hōji and kuyō offers practice in the art of attending to one's inner life with the help of others, as ironic as that may seem. Practicing these rites has the potential for cultivating an attitude and habit of reverence, from which respect can most propitiously issue. Reverence, then, becomes the bedrock of one's own capacity for grieving and the proper place from which to support others in theirs. Within this most sacred capability, one further has the opportunity to learn receptivity, reciprocity, and the value and forms of responding to others in a deep, mutually gratifying communion of souls. Beyond dismissiveness or denial, dissociation and distraction, in the holy ground of reverence, one can best get beyond oneself. Instead of the grasping, dominating tendencies of the ego, which puts oneself above and beyond others rather than participating with those others, one can experience flow.

As I have tried to describe—and even prescribe—this practice and social custom, I have noted that while it doesn't rely on any particular faith tradition or set of beliefs, it does require a certain discipline: a kind of restraint in public gatherings that allows for the full experience of *feelings*, with the hope of avoiding their being acted out. This prevents the worst of behavioral release of that "coiled spring" of the "surplus and force of emotion" that attends all grieving and can so easily lead to less-than-optimal outcomes. It is my fervent hope and prayer that a critical mass of folks in the United States, taking up these practices and the constructive discipline and etiquette it commends, will offset the violence we are currently so beset by and contribute mightily to making the world safe for the sorrow that is all too abundant in our day.

I have tried to show how a long history of being bereft of bereavement aids in the dominant culture of North America, stemming from the time of Henry VIII, has left us "ritually adrift, metaphorically impoverished and existentially vexed," to once again quote famous Irish undertaker Thomas

Lynch. The structure, schedule, and sensibilities of the Japanese ritual system known as hōji and kuyō offer an alternative that is adaptable, congenial, both complex and simple enough to suit all situations and all sorts and conditions of loss, and to aid us in sharing the challenges of being human in the most profound and satisfying ways. With a few easy guidelines for engaging, the Japanese rituals offer us unparalleled resources. The implications of applying these resources and the potential they hold for healing what ails us as a culture are immense. This brief introduction is not meant to be exhaustive, but rather a starting point and an invitation to join in the effort to understand and flesh out the vast potential of these resources to cure what ails us. This ritual system promises to synthesize and fulfill the contributions of medicine, psychology, anthropology, and history, as well as storytelling, meaning-making, and a need to overcome isolation. Most of all, they provide the context and crucible for cultivating reverence, with all the benefits that reverence affords us, in being good friends and creating a wholesome culture. And, at last, in making the world safe for sorrow.

Acknowledgments

Writing can be a painfully solitary, self-absorbed preoccupation. It has, therefore, been with great joy, relief, amazement, and gratitude that I eventually reemerged—like the seventeen-year cicada—from a seemingly underground activity into the light of day and the gift of collaboration.

My current collaborators naturally come to mind first: Jen Glynn, Leah Pierre, Kristine Peyre-Ferry, Chelsea Richards, Emma Watson, Kimberlene Francis, Pam Nordberg, Adrian Morgan, and Steve Elizalde. But much patient heavy-lifting and empathic hand-holding was done by Erin Brown, and I am eternally grateful for the initial encouragement of the soft-spoken Lari Bishop. And I would be remiss not to mention the superstructure in which we all work, created by Clint Greenleaf and competently and inspiringly sustained by Tanya Hall and Carrie Jones.

I owe an enormous debt to Ray Hawkins for his careful reading of several drafts, his professional eye, kind critique, and candid self-disclosures—and for the accomplished companionship of our colleague Stephen Oyer-Owens. Other early readers were Henry Bachofer; Jim and Jane Murphy; Steve Bond; and the members of a writing group hosted by my colleague Mike Adams, which included Danielle Jaussaud, Charles Kruvand, Joan Muller, Nick Deuster, Marcella Robertson, Bob Matlock, and Michael Nachbar.

Jim Bentley pointed me in the direction of several seminal writers and texts and was a marvelous sounding board for me, along with his wife, Carol. Andy Gerhardt suggested Francis Weller's work, and Carolyn Ellis thought surely I knew of Dan Siegel, since what I was doing so closely approximated his own method. I did not, but now I do—and am grateful for it.

Frank Richardson and Stephen Kinney brought the work of René Girard to my attention; I often think of later chapters in this book as a modest attempt to operationalize some of the best of Girard's analysis of the scapegoat mechanism by using a key passage from the Confucian tradition as encouragement to see in our social interactions the possibility of retracting our projections and taking full responsibility for ourselves, with compassion and love.

Allen Cline and his wonderful staff kept me alive, amused, and well; Sara Kennedy kept me clothed; Patti Tauber and Kevin Kott kept me fed. Kamal and Meena Adhikary kept me solvent. Glynn Lewis and Brian McCrae kept me housed; Mike Halprin kept me inspired and, along with Brian McCrae, helped me see a new avenue for the principles promoted in these pages being taught. And Janet McKellar and her partner, Danielle, provided validation and encouragement at a particularly low point.

Before all these lovely collaborators came on the scene, the underground in which I toiled was also teeming with nutrients stemming from even earlier: the mentorship of Arthur Kleinman and Tu Wei-ming; Richard Niebuhr and his wife, Nancy; and the gracious hospitality of his daughter Sarah and son-in-law Lynn. John Carman—then head of the Department of Comparative Religion at Harvard Divinity School—was sweetly excited at the prospect of this work. And Mary Evelyn Tucker reassured me that my take on Japanese Confucianism was accurate—in the main!

Laying the groundwork for this experiment were my Japanese collaborators: the late Fukushima Keido, head abbot of Tofukuji in Kyoto; Hayasaki Yūko; my former husband and in-laws primarily; but also Kashiwagi Tetsuo, Eguchi Shigeyuki and his wife Kimiko, Mizuta Ichiro, and the late Taketomo Yasuhiko.

I'm struggling to find the words to express my profound thanks, most especially to the pilot project participants for their trusting me—and each other—with their grief, most of whom you've had a chance to meet in these pages. Some even allowed their actual names to be used, recognizing that doing so enhances the accuracy of the reader's grasp of their experience and the meaning to be gained in the "spiritual recycling" of it—the prospect that others' learning and growing is a great way to honor their own.

And for providing the space, encouragement, and help in setting up the pilot project—and for entrusting their precious parishioners to me— my Episcopal clergy brethren, who stepped up when my applications for grants all failed in the wake of the economic crash of 2008: the Revs. David Hoster, Jim Stockton, and Mike Adams.

Esther Quantrill deserves special mention as a stalwart, steadfast friend who, as an accomplished writer herself, "heard, understood, and held" with me the torture that writing can be, spurred me on, and wished me "courage!"

Some folks who've been an enormous support have told me they don't want or need acknowledgment in these pages, and there will be some I fear I forget to mention despite the degree to which I relied on them and they influenced me. Perhaps the metaphor of the lighthouse that the Japanese frequently cite explains this best: the area around the base of the lighthouse is darkest (despite being closest). In this, I hope you'll find some recognition, rejoice in the beam of light that you helped cast for the safety of so many, and feel the profundity of my thanks.

Basic Instructions for the Practice of Kuyō

f you're interested in trying the basic contemplative practice of kuyō, here are the simple instructions and ritual schedule I gave to the pilot project participants. As you'll see, they give the practitioner a lot of leeway to experiment and do what feels right within certain basic guidelines while still being linked with and fed by an ancient tradition.

Preparing the Space and Time	Conducting the Ritual	In Between Times
Set aside a space that will remain undisturbed, if possible, and that will allow you to kneel, sit, or stand in front of it.	Enter the space and time with the intention to notice whatever thoughts and feelings arise without judgment.	Make notes in a journal of the thoughts, feelings, and impressions that came to you during the ritual.

Preparing the Space and Time	Conducting the Ritual	In Between Times
Provide whatever you decide to use to mark the beginning and the end of the ritual by word or sound: for instance, a prayer, a bell, or a wooden block with a gammel. You can also simply clap your hands once or twice.	Begin with a sound or prayer or gesture that demarcates the time and space: for instance, clap twice, ring a bell, bow, say a prayer, or sing a song.	Note any changes in your thoughts, feelings, or impressions.
Consider using candles and incense, placing a photo of the deceased at the altar, and making offerings of food and drink. Provide for safe use with adequate space around candles, something to catch dripping wax or falling ash, matches, or a lighter.	Address the deceased in whatever manner seems fitting to your mood of the moment, for instance: praise, complaint, tirade, lament, sadness, or longing.	Note if there are "action items:" things you want to clarify with others, questions about the deceased or oneself or the social milieu that others might answer, apologies that need to be made, adjustments in one's own behavior, requests for adjustments in behavior by others.
Prepare and place in the space some means of being reminded of a beautiful and benevolent dimension of life: prayer, song, sutra, or artwork.	Stay at the ritual space until it feels right to leave it, knowing you can return at the next opportunity. You need not achieve a completely peaceful sensation, but wait until it feels as though you are finished with what you have to say, feel, and think for the time being. Blow out candles.	Offer these thoughts, feelings, and impressions in the next ritual event and see what transpires.
	End with a bow, claps, bell, or prayer.	Consult with The Rite Source about things you might question.

RITUAL SCHEDULE

Daily, Weekly, and Yearly
Daily: Once or twice a day, morning and evening
Weekly: Once a week for the first seven weeks
The forty-ninth day (end of official mourning)
On the hundredth day after death
First anniversary
Second anniversary (counted as third event)
Sixth; twelfth; sixteenth; twenty-second; twenty-fourth or twenty-sixth; thirty-third; fiftieth; and every fifty years thereafter (counted as the seventh, thirteenth, seventeenth, twenty-third, twenty-fifth, twenty-seventh, thirty-third, and fiftieth anniversary events)
Monthly anniversary (e.g., the seventh day of each month)

APPENDIX B

✺

Permission to Regress in Order to Grow

When I first arrived in Tokyo decades ago, I stood at the top of the stairs at Tokyo Station staring down at a bustling crowd of black-haired people, all darting about. And I understood vectors for the first time: beginning at an arbitrary but distinct point in space and moving in a solid line from there—as if there had been no previous movement, no oscillation, nor any backward movement at all.

This is how I feel that most of us in the United States go through life: not allowing for even the slightest regression or wavering, dedicated to a linear way of thinking that underscores notions of "progress" and our commitment to it. This makes grieving, with its inevitable waves, oscillations, and outright regressive-feeling moments, particularly unbearable for us as Americans. We fear it (recall Mariah's dread of being inundated with sorrow again, having felt she'd finally "mastered" it); judge ourselves harshly for how we grieve (an often-unuttered but deep feeling of "What's wrong with me?"); and don't want to admit our struggles with grief to our friends who, even if they heard us, would not know how to support it. We may even disavow the emotions of grief—dissociate from it—to our peril.

Enter the stylized walking of the actors of Noh drama, the thirteenth-century Japanese theatrical form. These actors emerge from stage left to move across a lengthy pathway to the main stage, which juts out into the audience, where the central action of the play takes place. Their walk uncannily replicates, in an exaggerated but precise way, the exact way in which we connect with the earth in each step that we take—and what happens *to* the earth as we do so. It goes like this:

The actor pulls his foot slightly behind the other one and then moves it in a smooth arc past the stationary foot to place the first foot slightly ahead of the still one. This is emblematic of the way our foot pushes against the earth, and in so doing, moves *with* the earth, ever so slightly *backward*. The other foot now carries out the same motion, first moving slightly behind the now stationary foot before completing the forward motion in an arc past it. And so on.

Cognitive neuroscientists and parents everywhere, as well as sensitive adults who have tended to their own growth over a lifetime, will recognize this as the necessary regression before a moment of growth occurs. I first learned about this regression as an essential part of growth from human development researcher Kurt Fischer. His diagrams of a child's development were stair-like and entailed a little regression before a big leap up into higher levels of abstract thinking, as well as a move forward in time. I saw the regression as a need to get a running start for the big leap up![1] Freud spoke decades ago about "regression in the service of the ego"—that is, the necessary return to an earlier ego state in order to integrate an insight and be able to function in a way that incorporates the it.

I often tell people who talk to me about their agonizing moments of regression about this metaphor. It is universally received gratefully. And now you have it at your disposal—to help make sense of, and build a reverent receptivity to, the regressions we all need in order to grow.

Confucian Wisdom About Processing Emotion

"If you want something to contract,
first you must let it fully expand!"[2]

And, conversely,

"The way to expansion leads through contraction."[3]

For me, these two tropes describe the need for one to deal with the surplus and force of emotion entailed in grieving to allow one's feelings to expand—or to wait patiently until one has felt it all, without prematurely closing things down or dismissing them outright. This precludes, of course, *acting* on them and *only* prescribes the patience necessary for becoming aware of it all. In so doing, we are freed from the danger of being sabotaged by our emotions that exist in an unseen and unattended place in one's heart and mind.

On the other hand, one might also need a bit of cocooning or withdrawing and shrinking from one's activities to provide enough space and time for the "small, still voice" of all of their feelings to be heard, understood, and held. And in that, one should be free to expand into those feeling realms. Having a designated space and time to allow the feelings to well up can be helpful—and this is where kuyō comes in. Gathering with others at hōji events can also allow feelings to emerge that one may have been too shy or fearful to face alone.

Signs One Is Learning to Be Led

Psychoanalyst and spiritual director **Gerald G. May,** in *The Dark Night of the Soul*, compassionately explains the experience of learning to be led. He describes how the journey can initially make one feel lazy, inept, or simply bad. Do you relate to any of these experiences?

> Sometimes we may experience it as an inner relaxation and letting go. At other times it may feel like something we cling to is being ripped away from us. Either way, the freedom comes only through relinquishment. The actual experience may feel like delightful liberation or tragic bereavement, or it may happen so deeply that we are not aware of it at all. But one thing is certain: the process of freedom is one of subtraction—we are left more empty than when we began.[1]

Readers familiar with Japanese Buddhist concepts will recognize in May's diction of "relinquishment" the Japanese notion of *akirame*, one of the prime emotional experiences cultivated in their love of the cherry blossom. The blossoms' fleeting beauty inspires the capacity to enjoy their short-lived splendor and the capability of letting go.

May finally offers these three signposts that John of the Cross cited as markers of being on the right path:

1. "Drying up of gratifications and the powerlessness to do anything about it."[2]

2. "Lack of deep-down motivation to return to the old ways" ("they just don't hold the promise they once did").[3]

3. "Deep heartfelt desire within the community or group to 'remain alone in the loving awareness of God . . . in interior peace and stillness, without the acts and exercises.'"

May doesn't know what to make of this third sign, especially given people's lives in "marriage, in a corporation, in a nation" as contexts of those lives, making this third sign to May "incomprehensible."[4] Here, I find Meister Eckhart's interpretation of the Martha and Mary story helpful, that Martha, as the mature woman, has become able to remain in union with the godhead *while* serving. Martha was carrying on acts and exercises, unlike Mary, who, for a time, had to sit at Jesus's knee to learn and grow in that capacity and competence.

May is keen to state one other paradox: While markers along the way help us know if we're on the right track, one can never really know.

Finally, May would likely agree with Richard Rohr, who observes that the "ego hates to lose—even to God"![5]

Notes

INTRODUCTION

1. Johann Hari, *Lost Connections: Uncovering the Real Causes of Depression—and the Unexpected Solutions* (Bloomsbury, 2018), 79.

2. Hari, *Lost Connections*, 79.

3. Vivek H. Murthy, *Together: The Healing Power of Human Connection in a Sometimes Lonely World* (HarperCollins, 2020).

4. Vivek H. Murthy: "Surgeon General: Why I'm Calling for a Warning Label on Social Media Platforms," *New York Times* Guest Essay, June 17, 2024, https://files.commons.gc.cuny.edu/wp-content/blogs.dir/34827/files/2024/10/Social_Media_Packet.pdf.

5. Hari, *Lost Connections*, 80.

6. Hari, *Lost Connections*, 80.

7. Hari, *Lost Connections*, 80.

8. Marian Osterweis, Fredric Solomon, and Morris Green, eds., *Bereavement: Reactions, Consequences, and Care* (National Academy Press, 1984).

9. Osterweis, Solomon, and Green, *Bereavement*, 292–93.

10. "Surplus of emotion" was coined by Alexander and Margarete Mitscherlich in *The Inability to Mourn: Principles of Collective Behavior*, Beverley R. Placzek, trans. (Grove Press, 1975). Originally published in German as *Die Unfahikeit zu Trauern, Brundlglage kollectiven Verhaltens*, 1967, and the "force of emotion" by Renato Rosaldo in "Grief and a Headhunter's Rage: On the Cultural Force of Emotions," in *Text, Play and Story: The Construction and Reconstruction of Self and Society*, S. Plattner and E. Brunner, eds. (American Ethnological Society, 1984), 178–95.

11. E. O. Wilson. "Biologist E.O. Wilson on Why Humans, Like Ants, Need a Tribe." *Newsweek*, April 2, 2012, https://www.newsweek.com/biologist-eo-wilson-why-humans-ants-need-tribe-64005.

12. Hari, *Lost Connections*, 90.

13. Joe Yamamoto, Keigo Okonogi, Tetsuya Iwasaki, and Saburo Yoshimura, "Mourning in Japan," *American Journal of Psychiatry* 125, no. 12 (1969): 1660–65.

CHAPTER 1

1. Francis Weller, *The Wild Edge of Sorrow: Rituals of Renewal and the Sacred Work of Grief* (North Atlantic Books, 2015).

2. Stephen Greenblatt, "Hamlet in Purgatory," unpublished paper presented at the Medical Anthropology and Cultural Psychiatry Research Seminar, Harvard University, December 3, 1999, under the title, "The Supplication of Souls: Death and the Institutions of Grief."

3. Richard Fenn, *The Persistence of Purgatory* (Cambridge University Press, 1995).

4. Thomas Lynch, "Mourning in America," review of Sandra M. Gilbert, *Death's Door: Modern Dying and the Ways We Grieve, New York Times* Book Review, February 26, 2006, https://www.nytimes.com/2006/02/26/books/review/mourning-in-america.html.

5. Beverley Raphael, *The Anatomy of Bereavement* (Basic Books, 1983).

6. Philippe Ariès, *The Hour of Our Death*, Helen Weaver, trans. (Oxford University Press, 1981).

7. Ariès, *The Hour of Our Death*, 219–21.

8. Greenblatt, *Hamlet in Purgatory* (Princeton University Press, 2004), 102–3.

9. Greenblatt, *Hamlet in Purgatory*, 247.

10. Thomas Lynch, "Mourning in America."

11. Fenn, *The Persistence of Purgatory*, 22.

12. Fenn, *The Persistence of Purgatory*, 184.

13. Fenn, *The Persistence of Purgatory*, 30.

14. Baron Nobushige Hozumi, *Ancestor-Worship and Japanese Law*, originally published in 1912, 6th ed., revised by Shigeto Hozumi (Hokuseido Press, 1940).

15. Fenn, *The Persistence of Purgatory*, 186.

16. Charles Dickens, *American Notes for General Circulation* (Penguin, 1985), 285, cited in Richard Fenn, *The Persistence of Purgatory*, 169.

17. Rollo May, *Power and Innocence: A Search for the Sources of Violence* (W. W. Norton, 1972), 168–69.

18. Dickens, *American Notes*, in Fenn, *The Persistence of Purgatory*, 160.

19. Dickens, *American Notes*, in Fenn, *The Persistence of Purgatory*, 170.

20. Thomas Lynch, "Mourning in America."

21. Drew Gilpin Faust, *This Republic of Suffering: Death and the American Civil War*, (Vintage, 2009), 103.

22. Faust, *This Republic of Suffering*, 179.

23. Faust, *This Republic of Suffering*, 271.

24. Sigmund Freud, "Mourning and Melancholia" in Peter Gay, ed., *The Freud Reader* (W. W. Norton, 1989), 584–89, https://archive.org/details/petergay1989freudreader/Adam%20Phillips%20%5B2006%5D%20Penguin%20Freud%20Reader/page/n213/mode/2up.

CHAPTER 2

1. Ruth Davis Konigsberg, *The Truth About Grief: The Myth of Its Five Stages and the New Science of Grief* (Simon & Schuster, 2011).

2. Wesley Carr, *Brief Encounters: Pastoral Ministry through Baptisms, Weddings and Funerals* (SPCK Publishing, 1994).

3. Nicholas Peter Harvey, *Death's Gift: Chapters on Resurrection & Bereavement* (William B. Eerdmans, 1985).

4. Megan Devine, "The Five Stages of Grief and Other Lies That Don't Help Anyone," *HuffPost*, updated February 10, 2014, https://www.huffpost.com/entry/stages-of-grief_b_4414077.

5. *What's Your Grief?* (website) https://whatsyourgrief.com.

6. Sigmund Freud, "Mourning and Melancholia" in Peter Gay, ed., *The Freud Reader* (W. W. Norton, 1989), 584–89.

7. Robert Hertz, "A Contribution to the Study of the Collective Representation of Death" (1907), published with "The Pre-Eminence of the Right Hand: A Study in Religious Polarity" (1909) as *Death and the Right Hand*, ed. Rodney and Claudia Needham (Free Press, 1960) with introduction by E.E. Evans-Pritchard, https://en.wikipedia.org/wiki/Robert_Hertz.

8. Peter Gay, *The Freud Reader* (W. W. Norton, 1989). Also noted in Robert Kenny, "Freud, Jung and Boas: The Psychoanalytic Engagement with Anthropology Revisited," *The Royal Society Publishing: Notes and Records* 69, no. 2 (2015), https://doi.org/10.1098/rsnr.2014.0048.

9. Hertz, "A Contribution to the Study," 21.

10. Erich Lindemann, article in *American Journal of Psychiatry* 132, no. 3 (1975), https://doi.org/10.1176/ajp.132.3.296.

11. Eva K. Rosenfeld, "The Fire That Changed the Way We Think About Grief," *Harvard Crimson*, updated November 29, 2018, www.thecrimson.com/article/2018/11/29/erich-lindemann-cocoanut-grove-fire-grief/.

12. Rosenfeld, "The Fire That Changed."

13. Elisabeth Kübler-Ross, *On Death and Dying: What the Dying Have to Teach Doctors, Nurses, Clergy and Their Own Families* (Macmillan, 1969).

14. Ernest Becker, *The Denial of Death* (Simon & Schuster, 1973).

15. Becker, *The Denial of Death*, 284.

16. Becker, *The Denial of Death*, 285.

17. Marian Osterweis, Fredric Solomon, and Morris Green, eds., *Bereavement: Reactions, Consequences, and Care* (National Academy Press, 1984).

18. Osterweis, Solomon, and Green, *Bereavement*, 289–93.

19. Arthur Kleinman, *The Illness Narratives: Suffering, Healing, and the Human Condition* (Basic Books, 1988).

20. Colin Murray Parkes, *Bereavement: Studies of Grief in Adult Life, 3rd ed.* (International Universities Press, Inc., 1998); Osterweis, Solomon, and Green, *Bereavement*, 268.

21. John Bowlby and Colin Murray Parkes, "Separation and Loss Within the Family," in E. James Anthony and Cyrille Koupernik, eds., *The Child in His Family* (Wiley, 1970), 197–216; cited in Collin Murray Parkes, "A Historical Overview of the Scientific Study of Bereavement," in Margaret S. Stroebe, Robert O. Hansson, Wolfgang Stroebe, and Henk Schut, eds., *Handbook of Bereavement Research: Consequences, Coping and Care* (American Psychological Association, 2001), 29–30.

22. Parkes, "A Historical Overview," 35.

23. Janet T. Spence, "Achievement American Style: The Rewards and Costs of Individualism," *American Psychologist* 40, no. 12 (1985): 1285–95; Fred Rothbaum, John Weisz, Martha Pott, Kazuo Miyake, and Gilda Morelli, "Attachment and Culture: Security in the United States and Japan," *American Psychologist* 55, no. 10 (2000): 1093–1104.

24. Ian Suttie, *The Origins of Love and Hate* (Julian Press, 1935), ii.

25. Hari, *Lost Connections: Uncovering the Real Causes of Depression—and the Unexpected Solutions* (Bloomsbury, 2018), 90.

26. Parkes, "A Historical Overview," 26.

27. Renato Rosaldo, "Grief and a Headhunter's Rage: On the Cultural Force of Emotions," in *Text, Play and Story: The Construction and Reconstruction of Self and Society*, S. Plattner and E. Brunner, eds. (American Ethnological Society, 1984), 178–195. And Alexander and Margarete Mitscherlich, *The Inability to Mourn: Principles of Collective Behavior*, Beverley R. Placzek, trans. (Grove Press, 1975). Originally published in German as *Die Unfahikeit zu Trauern, Brundlglage kollectiven Verhaltens*, 1967.

28. Suttie, *The Origins of Love and Hate*, 4.

29. Ruth Benedict, *The Chrysanthemum and the Sword: Patterns of Japanese Culture* (World Publishing, 1946), 233.

30. Benedict, The *Chrysanthemum and the Sword*, 234–35.

31. Cary F. Baynes, trans., *The I Ching or Book of Changes (Bollingen Series)* (Princeton University Press, 1967), 463.

32. R. A Neimeyer, ed., *Meaning Reconstruction and the Experience of Loss* (American Psychological Association, 2001).

33. Margaret Stroebe and Henk Schut, "The Dual Process Model of Coping with Bereavement: Rationale and Description," *Death Studies* 23, no. 3 (1999): 197–224, https://doi.org/10.1080/074811899201046.

34. "Worden's Four Tasks of Mourning," Ourhouse Grief Support Center, https://www.ourhouse-grief.org/grief-pages/grieving-adults/four-tasks-of-mourning/.

35. Francis Weller, *The Wild Edge of Sorrow* (North Atlantic Books, 2015).

CHAPTER 3

1. Karl Goodkin et al., "Physiological Effects of Bereavement and Bereavement Support Group Interventions," in Margaret S. Stroebe, Robert O. Hansson, Wolfgang Stroebe, and Henk Schut, eds., *Handbook of Bereavement Research: Consequences, Coping and Care* (American Psychological Association, 2001), 678.

2. Private conversation, Yodogawa Christian Hospice, Osaka, Japan, July 2000.

3. The Rt. Rev. Charles Bennison, sermon on Isaiah 40:1, Memorial Church of Harvard University, c. 1997.

4. Mark Epstein, *Open to Desire: Embracing a Lust for Life* (Gotham Books, 2005), 147.

5. A transcript of a close variation of this explanation may be found at "Transcript of Walter Wink's Nonviolence for the Violent," Lutheran Peace Fellowship, transcript of a talk given in Louisville, Kentucky, June 13, 2001, https://www.lutheranpeace.org/articles/transcript-of-walter-winks-nonviolence-for-the-violent/. I heard the interpretation I cite in a sermon by an associate priest at Christ Church Cranbrook, Bloomfield Hills, MI, in the early 2000s.

6. Jonathan Haidt, "Why the Past 10 Years of American Life Have Been Uniquely Stupid," *The Atlantic*, April 11, 2022, https://www.theatlantic.com/magazine/archive/2022/05/social-media-democracy-trust-babel/629369/.

7. Daniel J. Siegel, *The Mindful Brain: Reflection and Attunement in the Cultivation of Well-Being* (W. W. Norton, 2007), 15–16 *(re COAL)*.

8. Catherine LaCugna, *God for Us: The Trinity and the Christian Life* (HarperSanFrancisco, 1993) in Richard Rohr, *The Divine Dance: The Trinity and Your Transformation* (Whitaker House, 2016), 194.

9. Gerald G. May, *The Dark Night of the Soul* (HarperOne, 2005).

10. Thomas Joiner, *Mindlessness: The Corruption of Mindfulness in a Culture of Narcissism* (Oxford University Press, 2017), 6.

11. Joiner, *Mindlessness*, 1.

12. Joiner, *Mindlessness*, 2.

13. Rollo May, *Power and Innocence: A Search for the Sources of Violence* (W. W. Norton, 1972), 168.

14. Ernest Becker, *The Denial of Death* (Simon & Schuster, 1973), quoting poet Rilke, 284.

CHAPTER 4

1. Keido Fukushima, *Mushin no Satori (Enlightenment of the Free Mind)* (Shinjusha, 1998).

2. Sigmund Freud, "Mourning and Melancholia" in Peter Gay, *The Freud Reader* (W. W. Norton, 1989), 584–89.

3. William James, *The Varieties of Religious Experience* (Longmans, Green & Co., 1928).

4. Gerald G. May, *The Dark Night of the Soul* (HarperOne, 2005), 78.

5. Francisco Varela, Evan Thompson, and Eleanor Rosch, *The Embodied Mind: Cognitive Science and Human Experience* (MIT Press, 2017), 246.

6. Varela, Thompson, and Rosch, *The Embodied Mind*, 246.

7. Simon Leys, trans., *The Analects of Confucius* (W. W. Norton, 1997), 31.

8. Leys, *The Analects of Confucius*, 27.

9. May, *The Dark Night of the Soul*, 130–31.

10. May, *The Dark Night of the Soul*, 184.

11. Mark Epstein, *The Trauma of Everyday Life* (Penguin, 2014), 170–71.

12. John Hull, *What Prevents Christian Adults from Learning* (Hymns Ancient & Modern Ltd, 2012).

13. Richard Rohr, *What the Mystics Know: Seven Pathways to Your Deeper Self* (The Crossroad Publishing Company, 2015), 42.

14. Wayne Dyer, "Dr. Wayne Dyer, Wishes Fulfilled; The Forever Wisdom of Dr. Wayne Dyer; Part 1," posted November 3, 2016, by Richard Johnson, YouTube, 21:11–25:21, https://www.youtube.com/watch?v=-_6Gh6pn2Es.

15. Reinhold Niebuhr, *An Interpretation of Christian Ethics* (Harper & Brothers, 1935).

CHAPTER 5

1. Mark Epstein, *The Trauma of Everyday Life* (Penguin, 2014), 79.
2. Epstein, *The Trauma of Everyday Life*, 108.
3. Epstein, *The Trauma of Everyday Life*, 197. Use of the term "relational home" is footnoting Robert Stolorow's *Trauma and Human Existence: Autobiographical, Psychoanalytic, and Philosophical Reflections* (Routledge, 2007), 10.
4. Epstein, *The Trauma of Everyday Life*, 73.
5. Epstein, *The Trauma of Everyday Life*, 73.
6. Rollo May, *Power and Innocence: A Search for the Sources of Violence* (W. W. Norton, 1972), 177.
7. Richard Rohr, *The Divine Dance: The Trinity and Your Transformation* (Whitaker House, 2016), 177.
8. Ian Suttie, *The Origins of Love and Hate* (Julian Press, 1935), 212.
9. Epstein, *The Trauma of Everyday Life*, 178.
10. Epstein, *The Trauma of Everyday Life*, 148.
11. Quoted in Rollo May, *Power and Innocence*, 125–26. May goes on to say that "parents who try to avoid children having games of aggression tend to create the very thing they think they're steering clear of."

CHAPTER 6

1. John O'Donohue, *Beauty: The Invisible Embrace* (HarperCollins, 2005), 24.
2. Paul Woodruff, *Reverence: Renewing a Forgotten Virtue* (Oxford, 2001), 209.
3. O'Donohue, "The Inner Landscape of Beauty," in interview with Krista Tippett, *On Being*, original air date February 28, 2008, https://onbeing.org/programs/john-odonohue-the-inner-landscape-of-beauty/.
4. O'Donohue, *Beauty*, 24.
5. Francis Weller, *The Wild Edge of Sorrow* (North Atlantic Books, 2015); O'Donohue, *Beauty*, 24.
6. O'Donohue, *Beauty*, 31.
7. Woodruff, *Reverence*, 180.
8. Woodruff, *Reverence*, 182.
9. Simon Leys, trans., *The Analects of Confucius* (W. W. Norton, 1997), 31.
10. Weller, *The Wild Edge of Sorrow*, 4.
11. O'Donohue, *Beauty*, 24; Mark Epstein, *The Trauma of Everyday Life* (Penguin, 2014).

12. Dennis Overbye, "Just a Few Billion Years Left to Go," review of Brian Greene's *Until the End of Time: Mind, Matter, and Our Search for Meaning in an Evolving Universe*, New York Times Book Review, updated March 4, 2020, https://www.nytimes.com/2020/02/17/books/review/until-the-end-of-time-brian-greene.html.

13. Suttie, *The Origins of Love and Hate*, 80.

14. Woodruff, *Reverence*, 179–80.

15. Ruth Ozeki, *A Tale for the Time Being* (Penguin, 2013), 189–92.

16. Citing a 2016 Silicon Valley talk by Dacher Keltner, UC Berkeley psychology professor and author of *Born to be Good: The Science of a Meaningful Life* (W. W. Norton, 2009), in Susan Cain, *Bittersweet: How Sorrow and Longing Make Us Whole* (Crown, 2022), 21.

CHAPTER 7

1. Paul Woodruff, *Reverence: Renewing a Forgotten Virtue* (Oxford Press, 2014), 50.

2. Susan Cain, *Bittersweet: How Sorrow and Longing Make Us Whole* (Crown, 2022), 21.

3. Woodruff, *Reverence*, 42-3.

4. Richard Fenn, *The Persistence of Purgatory* (Cambridge University Press, 1995), 22.

5. Riane Eisler, *The Chalice and the Blade: Our History, Our Future* (HarperCollins, 1988).

6. Leys, *The Analects of Confucius*, 15.

7. Richard Rohr, *Falling Upward: A Spirituality for the Two Halves of Life* (Jossey-Bass, 2011), 47.

CHAPTER 8

1. Richard R. Niebuhr, "Pilgrims and Pioneers," *Parabola* 9, no. 3 (1984); personal communication, September 17, 2016.

APPENDIX B

1. Kurt Fischer, *Human Behavior and the Developing Brain*, a course offered through the Mind, Brain, and Behavior curriculum at Harvard Graduate School of Education, Spring 2002. Some of the material taught in that class can be found in Geraldine Dawson, Kurt W. Fischer, eds., *Human Behavior and the Developing Brain* (Guilford Press, 1994).

2. This saying is actually attributed to Lao-Tse, the Taoist sage and author of the *Tao Te Ching*, but is quoted by Cary Baynes, *The Book of Changes*, 127.

3. Baynes, *The Book of Changes*, 463.

APPENDIX C

1. Gerald G. May, *The Dark Night of the Soul* (HarperOne, 2005), 87.

2. May, *The Dark Night of the Soul*, 178.

3. May, *The Dark Night of the Soul*, 178.

4. May, *The Dark Night of the Soul*, 178–79.

5. Richard Rohr, *Falling Upward: A Spirituality for the Two Halves of Life* (Jossey-Bass, 2011), 47.

Index

About the Author

The Rev. Dr. Margaret (Maggie) Izutsu spent much of her early adulthood in Japan, both during her undergraduate degree at Oberlin College and after graduating with a BA in East Asian Studies, as well as following her work as program director for the Mental Health Association of Washington in 1979–1980. She married into the culture and did most of her training there as a psychotherapist, helping found The International Counseling Centre in Kobe. She also worked as a translator, interpreter, teacher, editor, TV talent, and negotiator, serving in government, the media, and the private sector.

She returned to the States in 1990 to train for and enter the ministry as a third-generation Episcopal priest. After earning her MDiv at Harvard Divinity School, she went on to do a doctorate there in comparative religion. Serving on the faculty and administration of the Seminary of the Southwest brought her to Austin, Texas, in 2004, where, a few years later, she conducted a pilot project to see if Japanese memorial customs could be adapted for use in North America. She is the founder and CEO of The Rite Source, LLC, which provides counseling, education, and consultation and oversees an interactive website for individuals and groups of mourners, therapists, and other helping professionals and bereavement theorists to collaborate on offering better support for grief and spiritual development.